Insurance
Information
Institute

110 William Street
New York, N.Y. 10038
(212) 669-9200

P9-CES-617

# REINSURANCE:

# Fundamentals

# AND

# New Challenges

Ruth Gastel
Project Director

Sean Mooney, Ph.D.,
CPCU
Institute Economist
and Senior
Vice President
Planning and
Issues Analysis

Revised,
Second Edition

Second Edition, June 1989
First Edition, March 1983

Insurance Information Institute
110 William Street
New York, N.Y. 10038

ISBN 0-932387-20-9

# Contents

**FOREWORD**

5

**ACKNOWLEDGMENTS**

6

**EXECUTIVE SUMMARY**

7

**CHAPTER 1**

An Introduction to Reinsurance

11

**CHAPTER 2**

Reinsurance Marketing

28

**CHAPTER 3**

The Role of the Intermediary—
Leo T. Heifetz, E. W. Blanch Company

31

**CHAPTER 4**

Loss Development—Joseph W. Levin,
Employers Reinsurance Corporation

37

**CHAPTER 5**

Changes in the Reinsurance Environment—
Gerald F. Fisher, North American Reinsurance Corporation

59

*(continued)*

**CHAPTER 6**

Alien Reinsurance—Charles W. Havens III, and
William C. Marcoux, LeBoeuf, Lamb,
Leiby & MacRae, Attorneys
77


**CHAPTER 7**

Moving Center Stage: Reinsurance and Regulation
James L. Nelson, formerly with
Texas State Board of Insurance
83


**CHAPTER 8**

Recent Annual Statement Changes:
Improved Reinsurance Data—James M. Shamberger
Reinsurance Association of America
87


**GLOSSARY**

99


**SOURCES OF INFORMATION**

108


**INDEX**

109

# Foreword

NOT LONG AGO, reinsurance was a topic familiar only to practitioners—those in the insurance industry who were directly involved in reinsurance transactions—and almost unknown in business circles outside the insurance industry. Today, reinsurance is a subject of particular concern to those responsible for regulating the industry and also of increasing interest to the financial community as a whole.

With so much attention focused on the subject, it is not surprising that many people directly and indirectly involved in financial affairs—bankers, government officials, legislators, members of the press and others—are seeking to find out more about reinsurance.

To meet this interest, the Insurance Information Institute (I.I.I.) is publishing the second edition of this monograph. The I.I.I. for this edition asked a number of reinsurance experts to write articles and essays on the technical aspects of reinsurance for readers who are unfamiliar with the business. These essays, as a group, describe in simple terms what reinsurance is and how the industry functions and, in addition, give a broad overview of the new challenges facing the industry today.

The views and conclusions contained in this monograph are the opinions of the authors and do not necessarily reflect those of the members, directors or staff of the Insurance Information Institute.

Mechlin D. Moore, President
Insurance Information Institute

# Acknowledgments

The Insurance Information Institute is grateful to President Andre Maisonpierre and Senior Vice President James M. Shamberger of the Reinsurance Association of America for their help in developing and reviewing this monograph.

# Executive Summary

THIS MONOGRAPH IS PRESENTED in two sections—fundamentals of reinsurance and new challenges to reinsurers. The first chapter in the fundamentals section presents an overview of the reinsurance industry in a layperson's terms. The following chapters deal with the two basic elements of any reinsurance program—marketing and losses. The section dealing with new challenges contains four chapters—two that describe the changing environment in which reinsurers operate, one that addresses regulatory issues and one that explains the recent changes made in the annual financial statement filed with state regulators.

The first chapter, "An Introduction to Reinsurance," is a simple explanation of how reinsurance functions. It outlines the major differences between the two basic types of reinsurance—treaty and facultative. It goes on to discuss the differences between proportional and non-proportional forms of reinsurance as well as quota share, surplus share and excess-of-loss.

The second chapter deals with reinsurance marketing. It gives an overview of the two reinsurance distribution systems—the direct market and the brokerage market. (A direct writing reinsurance company deals directly with its customers. A broker, known in the business as an intermediary, brings the buyer and seller of reinsurance together.) The two segments of the market have similar approaches to the development of a reinsurance program, however their marketing strategies differ. The various phases involved in designing a program to meet a primary company's needs, including the detailed survey of company operations, are decribed by Leo T. Heifetz, senior vice president at E.W. Blanch, a reinsurance brokerage company. Mr. Heifetz emphasizes the concept of service and the need to maintain a continuous relationship with the client company.

The last chapter in the fundamentals section concerns losses. It covers an area known as loss development—the difference between the estimated cost of a loss as initially reported and the cost at final settlement. Author Joseph W. Levin, vice president and actuary, Employers Reinsurance Corporation, outlines the functions of claims and actuarial departments in terms of reserving for known and unknown losses. He discusses a study prepared by the Reinsurance Association of America (RAA) which shows reserve development patterns in various casualty or "long-tail" (slow loss emergence) lines.

Mr. Levin draws special attention to the fact that companies contributing data to the RAA study report that each year the "tail" is growing longer. He attributes this to various changing social and legal factors and warns that the results of this study have major implications for individual companies with regard to their loss reserve analyses. Mr. Levin compares reinsurer loss development patterns to those in primary companies, showing how inflation affects reinsurers to a much greater degree than primary insurers.

In the first chapter in the New Challenges to Reinsurers section, author Gerald Fisher, vice president and special counsel, North American Reinsurance Corporation, outlines the developments in the reinsurance business over the last few decades that, among other things, have led to changes in management philosophy and in reinsurers' traditional relationships with their ceding companies. These developments include increases in risk exposures; a shift from pro rata types of reinsurance to excess-of-loss; a greater focus on reinsurance by regulators; and the broad trends within the financial services industry which have affected all segments of this industry group.

The second chapter, Alien Reinsurance, by Charles W. Havens and William C. Marcoux, attorneys with LeBoeuf, Lamb, Leiby and MacRae, deals with the nature and size of the alien reinsurance market in the United States and how it operates. The chapter also discusses the changing regulatory climate for alien reinsurers which have been subject to special scrutiny in recent years. The authors touch on the legal and practical problems that legislators and regulators face in seeking to impose additional regulatory requirements on alien reinsurers.

The next chapter deals with the regulation of reinsurance. Reinsurance and Regulation: Moving Center Stage was written by James L. Nelson, former member, Texas State Board of Insurance and former chairman, Reinsurance and Anti-Fraud Task Force of the National Association of Insurance Commissioners. It provides some background on the regulation of the reinsurance business and suggests what direction future regulatory initiatives might take.

The severity of the downturn in the last insurance cycle focused attention on the financial condition of reinsurers and the need to improve the tools available to regulators to monitor solvency. The last chapter in this section, Recent Annual Statement Changes: Improved Reinsurance Data, by James M. Shamberger, senior vice president, Reinsurance Association of America, covers in detail various modifications to the annual financial statement and the reasons behind the changes. The new reporting formats will make it easier for regulators to determine whether an insurer has made adequate provision for losses not yet paid and whether a company is likely to have financial problems because its reinsurers have been slow to pay amounts due on reinsurance contracts.

# CHAPTER 1

# An Introduction to Reinsurance

REINSURANCE IS A FORM OF INSURANCE for insurance companies—a way of spreading the risk more widely. It enables one insurance company to assume part of the risk initially assumed by another insurance company. For example, under certain types of reinsurance contracts the primary or direct insurer transfers ("cedes") to the reinsurer a portion of the risk the primary company accepted in issuing (writing) insurance policies. In return for assuming the risk, the reinsurer receives a premium and agrees to indemnify the ceding company, according to a specific formula, for the cost of losses. This cost may include not only the amounts paid to the policyholder for claims covered by the policy, but also the administrative expense of adjusting the claims.

In many respects, the objective of reinsurance is similar to that of primary insurance: to remove some degree of financial uncertainty from the insured party. Just as primary insurance enables policyholders—drivers, owners of businesses and homeowners—to protect themselves against economic loss and manage their finances more effectively, reinsurance enables insurance companies to plan for contingencies more effectively. By limiting the liability they assume in issuing policies, reinsurance allows primary companies to provide greater amounts of insurance coverage on a direct basis.

Reinsurance contracts may follow the terms of the primary contract, but the original policyholder is not a party to the reinsurance contract. One of the reasons many people are unfamiliar with reinsurance is that the reinsurer generally does not have any direct relationship with, or legal obligation to, the original policy-holder. In fact, in most cases, the policyholder is unaware of the existence of the reinsurance contract. Reinsurance does not alter the primary insurer's responsibility to the policyholder. With or without reinsurance, the primary insurer is fully obligated to fulfill the terms of the policy it issued.

## FUNCTIONS OF REINSURANCE

Reinsurance performs five major, closely interrelated functions:
1. It increases a company's capacity to write policies for higher limits;
2. It enables an insurer to write a greater number of policies by reducing the size of the company's liabilities;
3. It helps to stabilize underwriting results;
4. It provides protection against catastrophic losses; and
5. It provides a form of financing by increasing policyholders' surplus, a technically complex concept that will be explained later.

## CAPACITY—INDIVIDUAL RISK

The first function of reinsurance is related to "underwriting capacity"—the maximum amount of insurance a company is able or prepared to write per policy and is related to the size of its policyholders' surplus.* Reinsurance increases this capacity.

Without reinsurance or some other mechanism for transferring liability, many companies would be severely restricted in the amount of coverage they could provide. Liability that could be assumed easily by a large insurance company—a policy covering an airline or a hospital, for example—might jeopardize the financial well-being of a smaller operation. This capacity gap between small and large

---

*The policyholders' surplus is roughly equivalent to the net worth of the company, which is defined as assets minus liabilities.

companies is reduced by reinsurance. When large "shock" losses are shared with the reinsurer, companies can write policies for higher limits. The increased capacity enables companies of various sizes to compete in the marketplace on a more equal footing.

## CAPACITY—PREMIUM VOLUME

By transferring some of the responsibility for the liabilities it has assumed, certain types of reinsurance allow a company (1) to write a greater number of policies, and (2) to cut down the maximum size of potential losses to a uniform level. As a result, the company can take better advantage of a mathematical principle known as the "law of large numbers," the cornerstone of insurance. In essence, the law of large numbers states that the more times an event is repeated, or the more units there are in a homogeneous group—automobile miles driven, houses insured in a geographical area and so on—the more predictable the outcome. Thus, the more policies of one type or class a company writes—supermarkets or automobile repair shops, for example—the more accurately it will be able to predict the statistical probability of loss in such establishments, and the closer the premiums will be to the actual cost of servicing this group of policyholders.

## STABILIZATION

Insurance companies also may purchase reinsurance for a third purpose: to stabilize results. (In the insurance industry, fluctuations in profit and loss are hard to avoid because insurance is a service or product that is sold before its actual cost is known.) Reinsurance can help stabilize results by controlling exposure to loss on individual policies and accumulated losses over a given period of time, and by reducing the risk involved in taking on new lines of insurance.

As mentioned earlier, reinsurance can be used to keep the maximum size of loss on individual policies to a manageable amount.

It also can be used to control accumulated losses. For example, some smaller companies may purchase reinsurance to mitigate the potential effect of a year of particularly poor underwriting results. Stated in simple terms, a company decides how much liability it is prepared to assume for any individual policy or the maximum amount of accumulated losses it can afford to sustain over a period of time, and reinsures everything above that limit. The amount of insurance a primary company keeps for itself or "retains" is known as the "net retained liability" or "net retention."

By enabling a company to limit the maximum amount of losses (individually and in the aggregate), reinsurance frees a primary insurer to move into new areas of business, a move that might be dictated not only by the needs of the insurance-buying public but also by the need to improve the mix of business. Diversification, especially geographic diversification, reduces the possibility that policyholders will suffer losses at the same time, a situation that could have a severe destabilizing effect.

But taking on new lines of insurance is fraught with risk. Lacking experience in a particular area, a company may have an inadequate data base from which to calculate proper rates and to establish appropriate underwriting policies. Information from the Insurance Services Office and other organizations that provide data and related services to the insurance industry is not available for all lines or types of business. In such circumstances, the primary insurer may look to the reinsurer for underwriting assistance, since the reinsurer may have experience in that or a related area.

However, while the risk transfer features and the other benefits of reinsurance can help a company entering a new field initially, it is not a substitute for proper underwriting. The benefits that reinsurance provides have to be weighed against its cost. The reinsurer, like the primary company, accepts a premium in return for assuming liability for losses which may or may not occur. It cushions the effects of insurer losses in the bad years but expects to receive an appropriate profit in the good years.

## PROTECTION AGAINST CATASTROPHES

Reinsurance also provides protection against catastrophic losses caused by man-made or natural disasters, such as riots, chemical spills or hurricanes. Even with an optimal geographic diversification of policyholders, a catastrophic event may cause huge losses, although losses sustained by individual policyholders may be relatively small. Without reinsurance, the impact of such catastrophic losses might be greater than the primary company could absorb.

## FINANCING

Reinsurance offers a form of financing by reducing the drain on policyholders' surplus, a situation that may occur in a company if premium volume is increasing rapidly. With certain types of reinsurance, the insurer receives a ceding commission from the reinsurer to cover acquisition expenses. This commission increases the policyholders' surplus.* The accounting mechanism that creates the need for reinsurance financing is described below in greater detail.

The cash flow chart (Diagram I) shows what happens to the premium when a policy is issued. To comply with statutory accounting requirements designed to assure a company's financial strength, the full amount of the premium initially must be put into the "unearned premium reserve" account. This amount is reduced and credited to earnings as the policy period progresses toward its expiration date. Funds in the unearned premium account cover a company's financial obligations to policyholders in the event of a policy cancellation. However, part of the premium already has been used to cover commissions, state taxes and other expenses incurred in acquiring the business. To balance accounts, insurers must take funds from another source, namely the policyholders' surplus.

------------------------------------------------------------

*A ceding commission always has an immediate, favorable impact on policyholders' surplus. However, in the long run, if the commission is insufficient to cover all acquisition expenses, future earnings will be unfavorably affected.

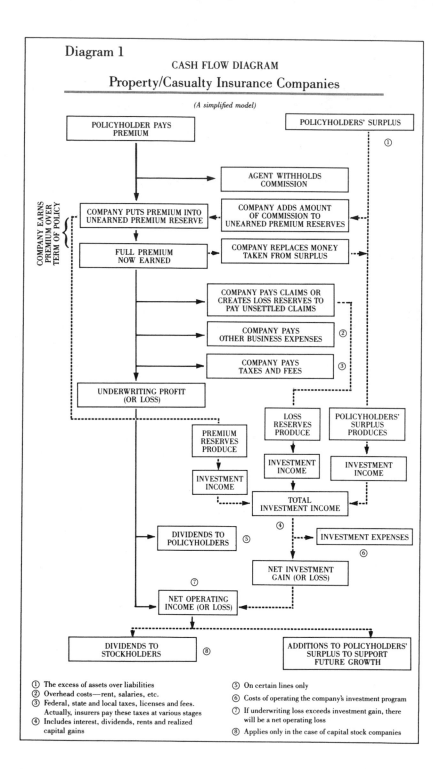

## Diagram 1

### CASH FLOW DIAGRAM
### Property/Casualty Insurance Companies

*(A simplified model)*

POLICYHOLDER PAYS PREMIUM

POLICYHOLDERS' SURPLUS ①

AGENT WITHHOLDS COMMISSION

COMPANY EARNS PREMIUM OVER TERM OF POLICY

COMPANY PUTS PREMIUM INTO UNEARNED PREMIUM RESERVE

COMPANY ADDS AMOUNT OF COMMISSION TO UNEARNED PREMIUM RESERVES

FULL PREMIUM NOW EARNED

COMPANY REPLACES MONEY TAKEN FROM SURPLUS

COMPANY PAYS CLAIMS OR CREATES LOSS RESERVES TO PAY UNSETTLED CLAIMS

COMPANY PAYS OTHER BUSINESS EXPENSES ②

COMPANY PAYS TAXES AND FEES ③

UNDERWRITING PROFIT (OR LOSS)

PREMIUM RESERVES PRODUCE

LOSS RESERVES PRODUCE

POLICYHOLDERS' SURPLUS PRODUCES

INVESTMENT INCOME

INVESTMENT INCOME

INVESTMENT INCOME

TOTAL INVESTMENT INCOME ④

DIVIDENDS TO POLICYHOLDERS ⑤

INVESTMENT EXPENSES ⑥

NET INVESTMENT GAIN (OR LOSS)

NET OPERATING INCOME (OR LOSS) ⑦

DIVIDENDS TO STOCKHOLDERS ⑧

ADDITIONS TO POLICYHOLDERS' SURPLUS TO SUPPORT FUTURE GROWTH

① The excess of assets over liabilities
② Overhead costs—rent, salaries, etc.
③ Federal, state and local taxes, licenses and fees. Actually, insurers pay these taxes at various stages
④ Includes interest, dividends, rents and realized capital gains

⑤ On certain lines only
⑥ Costs of operating the company's investment program
⑦ If underwriting loss exceeds investment gain, there will be a net operating loss
⑧ Applies only in the case of capital stock companies

If an insurance company is writing policies at a rapid rate, the need to balance accounts can result in a considerable drain on policyholders' surplus. This creates a problem because the state of an insurer's surplus account is a key measure of its financial health. Surplus serves as a backup to reserves in the event of unexpectedly severe losses, and also as a support for additional policies. Thus, failure to maintain an adequate policyholders' surplus can jeopardize future growth and ultimately, in an extreme case, lead to insolvency.

To lessen the negative effect of prepaid commissions described above, an insurer may decide to increase its policyholders' surplus through some form of financing. One way to raise such funds, in effect, is the use of reinsurance. As Diagram II illustrates, by purchasing reinsurance, a company decreases its liabilities. More importantly, as far as the financing function of reinsurance is concerned, by using pro rata reinsurance for a block of business, the ceding company receives a commission from the reinsurer as reimbursement for all or part of the primary insurer's expenses—agent commissions, underwriting and other business acquisition expenses. This payment increases surplus.

In the case illustrated in Diagram II, the company has improved the ratio of premiums to policyholders' surplus from 4:1 to 1.25:1 (a ratio of 3:1 generally is considered adequate), and the actual amount of surplus has increased from $2 million to $3 million. An increase in surplus improves other financial ratios, e.g., the ratio of assets to liabilities, and also allows for more favorable comparisons with prior periods (year or quarter).

## FORMS OF REINSURANCE

Reinsurance, as a business separate from primary insurance, had its beginnings in the 18th century, but it did not become a significant segment of the insurance industry until well into the 20th century. Then, as the insurance industry grew, new uses for reinsurance developed and new forms of reinsurance were created, each tailored to meet a particular need.

## Diagram II

## How Reinsurance Improves an Insurer's Financial Position

1. Insurer's balance sheet before reinsurance.

| | Assets | Liabilities and policyholders' surplus | |
|---|---|---|---|
| **Cash** | **$ 8,000,000** | **Unearned premium** | **$ 8,000,000** |
| **Other** | **$ 14,000,000** | **Other liabilities** | **$ 12,000,000** |
| | | **Policyholders' surplus** | **$ 2,000,000** |
| | **$ 22,000,000** | | **$ 22,000,000** |

$$\textbf{Ratio of premiums to surplus} = \frac{\$8,000,000}{\$2,000,000} = \textbf{4:1}$$

2. Insurer reinsures half (50%) of its business, $4,000,000, and receives a 30% ceding commission.

| | Assets | Liabilities and policyholders' surplus | |
|---|---|---|---|
| **Cash** | **$ 5,200,000\*** | **Unearned premium** | **$ 4,000,000** |
| **Other** | **$ 14,000,000** | **Other liabilities** | **$ 12,000,000** |
| | | **Policyholders' surplus** | **$ 3,200,000\*\*** |
| | **$ 19,200,000** | | **$ 19,200,000** |

**\*$8,000,000 less $4,000,000 in premiums plus $1,200,000 (30%) in ceding commission.**
**\*\*$2,000,000 original policyholders' surplus plus $1,200,000 ceding commission.**

$$\textbf{Ratio of premiums to surplus} = \frac{\$4,000,000}{\$3,200,000} = \textbf{1.25:1}$$

Results: 1. The ratio of premiums to surplus has improved from 4:1 to 1.25:1.
2. Surplus has increased from $2,000,000 to $3,200,000.

## BASIC TYPES OF REINSURANCE—TREATY AND FACULTATIVE

There are two basic kinds of reinsurance—"treaty" and "facultative." The term treaty reinsurance denotes a type of reinsurance that covers broad groups of policies—all of a company's business or policies of a particular type. Facultative reinsurance covers specific, individual risks.

In most treaty agreements, once the terms of the contract have been established, all policies that fall within those terms—both new and existing business in many cases—are covered under the agreement on an ongoing basis until the agreement is canceled. Depending on the type of cancellation, some coverage may even be provided for a period of time after cancellation.

With facultative reinsurance, however, the ceding company and the reinsurer must negotiate a specific agreement for each risk covered. This type of reinsurance frequently is used where the value of the property to be reinsured is higher or the operations more unusual or more hazardous than those covered by the reinsurance treaty, and where a careful appraisal of the hazards involved is required. It is called facultative because, in contrast to treaty reinsurance, the reinsurer retains the "faculty" or power to accept or reject all or part of any policy offered to it, and the insurer can choose whether to purchase reinsurance for a particular policy and, if so, when and from whom.

Facultative and treaty reinsurance agreements are classified as "pro rata" (proportional) or "excess-of-loss" (non-proportional) depending on the arrangement by which losses are apportioned. (See Diagram III.) In a pro rata agreement (most commonly applied to property coverages) the reinsurer assumes a predetermined share of the liability assumed under the original contract in return for a predetermined share of the policyholder premium, and the same share of any losses and expenses. The primary insurer's exposure to loss therefore is limited by the percentage of the policy or policies it cedes and the size of these policies. In an excess-of-loss agreement there is a "deductible." The primary insurer pays for all loss amounts within the net retention or deductible and the reinsurer for loss amounts in excess of or above that level.

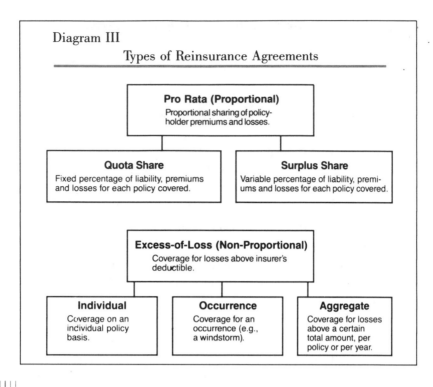

Diagram III
Types of Reinsurance Agreements

**Pro Rata (Proportional)**
Proportional sharing of policy-holder premiums and losses.

**Quota Share**
Fixed percentage of liability, premiums and losses for each policy covered.

**Surplus Share**
Variable percentage of liability, premiums and losses for each policy covered.

**Excess-of-Loss (Non-Proportional)**
Coverage for losses above insurer's deductible.

**Individual**
Coverage on an individual policy basis.

**Occurrence**
Coverage for an occurrence (e.g., a windstorm).

**Aggregate**
Coverage for losses above a certain total amount, per policy or per year.

## PRO RATA REINSURANCE AGREEMENTS

There are basically two types of pro rata plans: quota share and surplus share. Under a quota-share agreement, the insurer cedes a fixed percentage of each policy written in a certain line or class of business, and receives a commission from the reinsurer for the business ceded. Once the percentage has been decided, the division of premiums and any losses that occur is automatic. In a 65 percent quota-share agreement, for example, the primary insurer retains, or will pay for, 35 percent of any losses and the reinsurer assumes 65 percent of any losses covered by the contract in return for a proportionate amount of the original policyholder premium.

Under a surplus-share agreement, the primary insurer's retention is stated as a dollar amount. If the amount of insurance under a policy is less than the retention, no liability is ceded. If it is greater than the retention, the excess—the remainder of liability up to the liability limits—is reinsured. The premium is shared in the ratio of the retained liability to ceded liability.

Consider a policy with limits of $150,000 and a premium of

$1,500, for example. Under a surplus-share agreement with a retention of $25,000, the primary insurer will retain $25,000 and cede $125,000 to the reinsurer. The premium of $1,500 will be shared in proportion to the liabilities,

$$\text{i.e.,} \quad \frac{\$125,000}{\$\ 25,000} = 5{:}1$$

Losses are shared in the same proportion: 5:1. For example, for a loss of $100,000, the primary insurer would pay $16,667 and the reinsurer would pay five times that amount, or $83,333.

Diagram IV illustrates how quota and surplus-share reinsurance would apply to this transaction. The quota-share example is a 75 percent quota-share agreement in which the primary insurer retains 25 percent and cedes 75 percent to the reinsurer.

Diagram IV

Comparison of Quota-Share and Surplus-Share
Reinsurance

| | Quota Share | Surplus Share |
|---|---|---|
| Insurance Policy — **$150,000** | | |
| **Retention:** | **25%** | **$ 25,000** |
| Amount of Insurance — **$150,000** | | |
| **Insurer's share:** | **$ 37,500** | **$ 25,000** |
| **Reinsurer's share:** | **$ 112,500** | **$ 125,000** |
| **Total insurance:** | **$ 150,000** | **$ 150,000** |
| Amount of Premium — **$1,500** | | |
| **Insurer's share:** | **$ 375** | **$ 250** |
| **Reinsurer's share:** | **$ 1,125** | **$ 1,250** |
| **Total premium:** | **$ 1,500** | **$ 1,500** |
| Amount of Loss — **$100,000** | | |
| **Insurer's share:** | **$ 25,000** | **$ 16,667** |
| **Reinsurer's share:** | **$ 75,000** | **$ 83,333** |
| **Total losses:** | **$ 100,000** | **$ 100,000** |

Basically, the difference between quota and surplus share is in terms of the retention. Under quota-share the retention is a fixed percentage of each policy and under a surplus-share the retention is variable. This means that under a quota-share agreement, the percentage of liability stays the same for both parties regardless of the size of the policies covered. But under a surplus share, because the amount is fixed, the reinsurer's percentage of liability increases as the policy limits increase.

In surplus-share reinsurance, the insurer generally has the option to decide how much of each policy is to be ceded, subject to certain conditions that are set out in the agreement. As a result, there will be policies with 60 percent reinsurance protection, for example, and others with only 30 percent protection. Once the amount of reinsurance protection on a policy has been determined, all transactions flow proportionately.

The conditions set out in a surplus-share agreement usually focus on the size a policy has to be in order to be included in a surplus agreement, or, stated another way, the amount of liability that the ceding company wishes to retain. If the policy limits are greater than the insurer's retention, the "surplus" is ceded to the reinsurer. The limit of a surplus-share agreement or the maximum amount of liability a reinsurer is prepared to assume is normally expressed in terms of "lines." (A line is equal to the ceding company's retention.) So if an agreement is described as a "five-line surplus," for example, the reinsurer will assume coverage up to five times the primary company's retention amount.

## EXCESS-OF-LOSS REINSURANCE AGREEMENTS

In excess-of-loss or non-proportional plans, the ceding company is indemnified for the portion of a loss that exceeds a specified amount (the ceding company's net retention), subject generally to a fixed limit of reinsurance. In contrast to pro rata plans, the premium paid by the primary company for excess-of-loss reinsurance bears no proportional relationship to the original premium paid by the policyholder. It is a charge based on the potential for loss. Excess-of-loss agreements may cover policies on an individual basis. They also may apply to an occurrence—a tornado, for example—which enables the ceding company to recover losses associated with one catastrophic event in excess of a given total, losses that may involve many different policyholders. In addition, excess-of-loss agreements may be written to cover an aggregate of losses incurred over a period of time, usually a year. (See Diagram III.) Such contracts often are called "stop-loss" and "excess-of-loss ratio" reinsurance contracts. These and variations of the other basic forms of reinsurance outlined above have been devised to meet specific needs as they arise.

## LAYERING

Excess-of-loss reinsurance can be applied at various levels of liability and in combination with other types of reinsurance, as the following example shows.

Diagram V illustrates how layers of reinsurance might apply to a given policy. In this case, a primary insurer has issued a fire insurance policy on an industrial building to the Consolidated Widget Company. The structure has been built with fire resistive materials, and to further limit potential fire damage, a water sprinkler system and other protective devices have been installed. The primary company's limit of liability for the building is $20 million.

The policy is covered automatically under two of the company's existing reinsurance treaties. The primary company's first layer of reinsurance protection is a 90 percent quota-share treaty with Reinsurer A with a treaty limit of $500,000. Under this agreement the primary insurer's maximum exposure to loss is $50,000, or 10 percent of the treaty limit.

Consequently, if a fire caused $150,000 of damage, losses would be shared between the primary insurer and the reinsurer in proportion to the liability each has assumed under the terms of the treaty. The primary company would pay one-tenth or $15,000 of the loss and Reinsurer A would pay nine-tenths or $135,000.

The second reinsurance treaty is an excess-of-loss treaty with Reinsurer B which covers losses above $500,000 up to a limit of

$5 million. So if fire losses totaled $2 million, the primary insurer would pay $50,000, Reinsurer A would pay $450,000 and Reinsurer B would pay the remaining $1.5 million of loss.

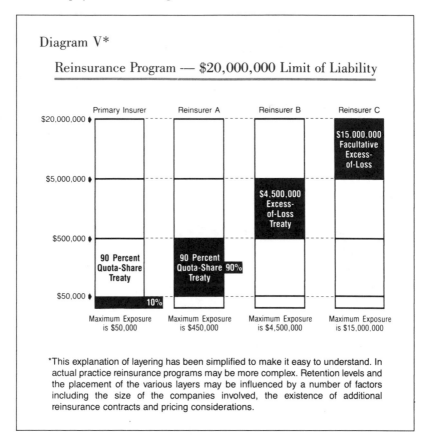

Diagram V*

Reinsurance Program — $20,000,000 Limit of Liability

*This explanation of layering has been simplified to make it easy to understand. In actual practice reinsurance programs may be more complex. Retention levels and the placement of the various layers may be influenced by a number of factors including the size of the companies involved, the existence of additional reinsurance contracts and pricing considerations.

The Consolidated Widget Company's fire insurance policy is for $20 million. The primary insurer therefore needs a third layer of reinsurance to cover the extremely remote possibility that losses would exceed $5 million. It decides to purchase excess-of-loss protection from one of its facultative reinsurers.

Facultative reinsurance coverage is not "automatic"—a separate contract is negotiated for each policy covered. Generally the reinsurer will make a detailed evaluation of the factors that might contribute to losses, in this case fire losses, and the measures that the primary insured, the widget manufacturer, has taken to control those hazards.

Since the Consolidated Widget Company's premises satisfy the reinsurer's underwriting criteria, Reinsurer C agrees to provide excess-of-loss coverage for losses above $5 million to the $20 million limit. In the event of a catastrophic loss that penetrated this last layer of protection, amounts would be apportioned as previously described except that Reinsurer B would pay $4.5 million, the full amount of its liability under the treaty, and Reinsurer C would pay for losses that exceeded $5 million up to the primary policy limit of $20 million.

The above is a hypothetical case. Reinsurance contracts are customized to deal with specific situations so that in real life this program may be modified in a variety of ways.

## HOW THE REINSURANCE INDUSTRY FUNCTIONS

Reinsurance is available from "professional" reinsurers (companies whose principal or sole business is reinsurance), from the reinsurance departments of primary companies and from various organizations such as reinsurance pools or syndicates, Lloyd's and government-owned companies.

Pools and syndicates, such as the Workers' Compensation Reinsurance Bureau, the Mutual Atomic Energy Reinsurance Pool and the Excess Bond Reinsurance Association (an organization that reinsures policies covering banks against employee dishonesty), are formed by groups of insurers that join together to reinsure each other, sometimes in areas that are extremely specialized or have a high loss potential. These pools offer another advantage. By pooling resources, members of the pool increase their capacity, which enables them to write primary insurance for higher amounts than they could provide individually. Terms governing the apportionment of loss vary. Some organizations require members to assume a certain percentage of every loss. Other arrangements are similar to an excess-of-loss agreement in which members take responsibility for their own losses up to a certain point. Losses exceeding the specified amount are then shared equally by all members of the pool. As an extra layer of protection, reinsurance may be purchased separately to protect the pool itself and to protect member companies for liability they assume as members of the pool.

## THE REINSURANCE MARKET

A primary insurer may deal directly with a reinsurance company or through a reinsurance intermediary, sometimes called a reinsurance broker. As independent contractors, intermediaries seek out the best available terms for their clients and are free to place business with any reinsurance company that deals with intermediaries, subject to the client's approval. Although intermediaries work on behalf of the ceding company, they are paid a commission by the reinsurers with which they place their clients' reinsurance business. Business is offered to a wide spectrum of the reinsurance market. Each potential reinsurer makes a commitment to accept a certain portion of the business. This amount may be reduced if total commitments exceed the amount to be reinsured. In this way, reinsurance company portfolios are balanced so that large single losses (other than catastrophic losses) have only a limited effect on individual reinsurers. To stabilize results further, reinsured business can be ceded to other reinsurance companies. This procedure is known as retrocession.

Reinsured business also can be exchanged between two companies in equal premium amounts or based on the potential profitability of the business to be exchanged. By trading a portion of its business that is subject to different conditions from the business it receives in return, a company can reduce the probable variation results. This form of diversification, call reciprocity, is not widely used in the United States but is common in other countries. It is, however, the oldest method of spreading risk and placing reinsurance.

A reinsurance program can be simple, involving just one form of reinsurance contract, such as a quota-share treaty. But where the limits of liability are high, programs may consist of several different types of reinsurance, both facultative and treaty agreements, as well as pro rata and excess, often shared among a number of reinsurers.

Industrywide, the treaty/facultative breakdown of premiums written varies from year to year with market conditions. On average, the ratio is about four (treaty) to one (facultative).

## RELATIONSHIP BETWEEN PRIMARY INSURER AND REINSURER

Reinsurers operate on the basis of a promise to pay just as primary insurers do. The traditional relationship between the primary insurer and the reinsurer is based on "good faith," a vestige of a less complex era when business deals were consummated with a handshake and backed with little more than a gentleman's reputation. Although reinsurance agreements nowadays are formalized in contracts, the contracts tend to be shorter than those used in other fields. There is no standard contract. Provisions, except those required by state law, reflect the varying needs of each party. Differences of opinion regarding contract interpretation normally are decided by arbitration panels composed of experienced insurance and reinsurance personnel rather than through litigation.

## LICENSING REQUIREMENTS

Regulation of the reinsurance industry traditionally has been limited, because it is viewed as a transaction between equals. A professional reinsurer domiciled in the United States must, however, meet statutory licensing requirements similar to those required of a primary company in the state in which it is applying for permission to do business. It also must meet solvency requirements, comply with general insurance laws and file the same annual statements and reports as a primary company. Laws governing some of the more technical aspects of reinsurance differ from state to state.

# Reinsurance Marketing

## AN OVERVIEW

I
N THE UNITED STATES, reinsurance is marketed primarily
through two distribution systems—the direct (non-brokerage)
market and the brokerage market.

The recent changes that have taken place in the reinsurance
market—the growth of the reinsurance business and the entry
of many new reinsurers—have blurred many of the distinctions that
formerly existed between the two marketing systems. Consequently, it
is difficult to make generalizations about the characteristics and
marketing strategies of direct writing reinsurers and intermediaries
and the reinsurers that do business in the brokerage market.

As far as buyers of reinsurance (ceding companies) are concerned,
decisions about which system to use depend largely on the size of the
company and the individual preferences and philosophy of its
management.

There are advantages to each method of distribution. The fact that
the two systems can exist side-by-side and flourish attests to the
strengths that each brings to the reinsurance marketplace.

## THE DIRECT WRITER

Direct writing reinsurers, or direct writers, operate through their
own salaried sales force, known as account executives. They maintain
a staff of underwriters, loss control specialists, actuaries, statisticians

and others capable of providing all the necessary technical services. The typical account executive has experience in a broad range of insurance company operations, particularly in the field of underwriting. This background, together with the in-house expertise available from the direct writing company, enables the account executive to serve the primary company in many respects as a consultant.

The placement of reinsurance with a direct writer is similar in some ways to the placement process described in "The Role of the Intermediary," the next article in this monograph. The account executive, like the intermediary, is the person who negotiates the terms and conditions of the reinsurance contract, and through whom all communications are channeled; who coordinates the activities and services that form part of the reinsurance program such as the interaction between the two companies' underwriting and claims departments; and who is responsible for steering the two parties on a course that will avoid major problems.

The two distribution systems are not alike in all respects, however. There are a number of important differences. One of the most obvious is that in the direct market, the assuming reinsurer and the provider of technical services are the same entity. This means that a primary company looking for assistance in such areas as underwriting, claims handling and taking on new lines of insurance can obtain those services from the same company that is assuming its reinsurance business. In effect, direct writing reinsurers provide "one-stop shopping."

The second difference is that a direct writer's account executives have the full authority of the reinsurer behind them. They can "bind" or commit the company to reinsurance contracts up to specific limits which may vary with the type of primary business and the reinsurance program required, the policy of the individual reinsurer, and the account executives' position with the company. In certain cases, account executives also have authority to settle claims. In addition, they can speak directly for the reinsurer on all matters concerning the reinsurance program.

According to some people in the reinsurance marketing field, there is a difference between an account executive's responsibility for the results of business he or she "produces," or brings into the company, and an intermediary's responsibility for results. While intermediaries depend on good results to maintain continuing relationships with reinsurers, the results of underwriting decisions made by account executives flow to their employers' bottom line. Because account executives are more directly accountable for the profitability of any reinsurance program, they take an active role in the underwriting process, personally approving terms and conditions, making recommendations on retrocessions (the ceding of reinsurance business to other reinsurers) and closely monitoring and evaluating underwriting results throughout the contract year.

The direct market attracts those that need the technical services the direct writing reinsurer can provide, that prefer to have direct contact and a one-on-one relationship with the reinsurer and that want to keep the number of companies they must deal with to a minimum. The direct writer's book of business therefore may include accounts from a wide range of primary companies of varying sizes.

However, because direct writers prefer to handle a ceding company's entire account or a large portion of it, a direct writer's target market generally is the small- to medium-sized primary insurer. The reinsurance needs of large primary companies usually exceed the capacity of any one reinsurer. As a result, large insurers tend to split their business among a number of different reinsurers.

The step-by-step process involved in putting together a reinsurance program is described in the following article.

# CHAPTER 3

# The Role of the Intermediary

By Leo T. Heifetz
Senior Vice President, E. W. Blanch Company

INTERMEDIARIES ARE THE MIDDLEMEN in reinsurance transactions. They bring buyer and seller together. Within this framework, the intermediary assumes many roles, at times the inquisitor, the devil's advocate, the diplomat, the referee, the accounting expert, the tax expert, the industry bellwether, the broad shoulder, the father confessor and, every once in a while, the fall guy.

An intermediary's function in the reinsurance transaction process can be divided chronologically into six different parts—contact, survey, conceptualization, authorization, placement and service.

## CONTACT

As in any other business there are a myriad of approaches ranging from the cold call to the referral and from the casual to the purely business approach. Generally, by careful study of the prospective company's annual "convention" statements (uniform annual financial statements required by all United States insurance jurisdictions, as prescribed by the National Association of Insurance Commissioners), financial material, such as stockholder reports, historical information and resumes, and by careful selection of reference material from these sources, an intermediary can create an opening.

## SURVEY

Having received permission to obtain all the data necessary to make recommendations regarding the company's reinsurance program, the intermediary sets out on a fact-finding mission. At the beginning of such a mission the broker usually outlines the information he or she requires and determines its availability.

The company seldom can supply all of the requested material. An area which is often troublesome is a limits profile. A limits profile is an array of the number of insured properties or operations by size; i.e., how many have limits of $100,000, $500,000 or $1 million, for example? It is important to have these data by number of policyholders and by premiums for each size category to determine what kind of reinsurance program is needed. If the company does not have this information in summary form, the intermediary must perform a sampling, physically examining a representative number of the company's policies (daily reports) to collate the desired data. In addition, the intermediary must determine the amount of time and the number of people needed to complete the sampling—communication of the sampling schedule is important to minimize disruption of the company's normal work routines—and must also establish guidelines for the project workers which will ensure equal and consistent recording of the data.

The survey becomes the intermediary's learning ground about the company. It enables the intermediary to make recommendations about the reinsurance program, to offer advice about improvements in specific areas of the company's operations and to answer prospective reinsurers' questions about the company. A good survey will encompass the following aspects of the company's operations:

A. Underwriting
B. Rate filings
C. Claims
D. Distribution of business
   1. By line
   2. By territory
   3. By limits

E.  Expenses
F.  Financial data
G.  Existing reinsurance
H.  Current philosophies
I.  Future plans

Some of the above items require explanation. "Rate filings" should include a study of the company's rates by state, in relation to those of its leading competitors. "Claims" includes a variety of possible survey areas including reserve adequacy, case inventory, rate of closings, number of cases by size, losses incurred but not reported (IBNR), and follow-up procedures with adjusters and attorneys. "Current philosophies" could include an analysis of the company's risk-bearing capabilities and, most importantly, management's attitude toward the assumption of risk. In other words, are production and underwriting goals in line with the company's financial position? This aspect may pertain to under- or over-utilization of capital.

## CONCEPTUALIZATION

After having completed the survey, the intermediary is in a position to make recommendations. These recommendations, which may range from a few minor adjustments to a major overhaul of the primary insurer's reinsurance program, should fit in with the company's current and future plans. For example, a company may decide to increase its insurance writings (sales) by entering (becoming licensed to do business in) new states or by filing new "products." It may be necessary to finance new ventures through the use of quota-share reinsurance. This may require a precise timetable, after which an excess-of-loss program may be employed. Often various combinations of basic reinsurance can be used to achieve a cost-effective means of reinsuring and to provide additional catastrophe protection, statement protection (improve the ratio of policyholders' surplus to liabilities, as shown on the annual statement), financial relief and capacity. The importance of this phase cannot be overestimated.

## AUTHORIZATION

At this point, assuming the recommendations are acceptable to management, the company gives the intermediary an order or a "broker-of-record letter," which is authorization to pursue the suggested program. In certain instances during the conceptualization phase, the company may authorize the intermediary to approach a few specific reinsurers, usually those which the intermediary has recommended, for the purpose of obtaining "lead" quotations.

## PLACEMENT

The intermediary should determine a placement strategy for the complete "subscription" of the program. In the brokerage market, seldom is 100 percent of a specific reinsurance program underwritten by a single reinsurer. Depending on the size of the company, the number of reinsurance contracts comprising a program can vary from one to dozens. For example, a catastrophe reinsurance program may consist of five layers and there may be a completely different cast of reinsurers on each layer. (See "An Introduction to Reinsurance" for an explanation of layering.) A skillful broker can search out those reinsurers interested in the lower layers and those interested in the higher layers. This flexibility enables the intermediary to obtain for the client company the most cost-effective reinsurance program.

To have some idea of whether a reinsurance contract is placeable and at what price, the intermediary must keep abreast of the direction of the market and know which reinsurers are interested in specific types of business.

Keeping up with the market can be a demanding task, particularly now that the pattern of insurance cycles appears to be changing. The last recovery was the shortest on record and, if present trends continue, the same conditions that marked the early 1980s are likely to prevail: overcapacity leading to depressed profits as the laws of supply and demand act to push prices down.

As the market moves from undercapacity, with fewer players and higher prices, to overcapacity, the intermediary must constantly monitor what is going on to protect market share. In such a market, continuity and financial responsibility also become major considerations. Which companies can be relied upon to remain in the market for the long term?

In addition to dealing with intricacies of an ever-changing marketplace, intermediaries must fulfill the requirements of outside agencies, such as certified public accountants and state insurance departments, to which they must furnish complete details of each reinsurer's finances. All of this increases the work and skill involved in the placement phase of the reinsurance transaction process.

## SERVICE

Having completed the designated program prior to its effective date, the intermediary writes to the primary company to confirm the terms and provides it with a list of the reinsurers with which business has been placed, along with their percentage participations. Immediately thereafter the intermediary submits a reinsurance contract describing the terms and conditions. The "wording," as the contract is often called, usually is sent to the reinsurers first for approval and execution (permission to carry out the agreed program). When all reinsurers to a particular contract have signed, it is then submitted to the primary company for similar action. Finally, fully executed copies are distributed to all parties.

It is the intermediary's responsibility to obtain all premium and loss accounts from the primary company and to distribute to each reinsurer copies of each premium transaction. The speed with which individual losses are collected and transmitted is paramount to establishing an aura of good service. The importance of this aspect of service cannot be overemphasized.

The intermediary endeavors to assure the timeliness of these reports and remittances and makes periodic checks for accuracy. The above are basic functions of the intermediary as respects each contract in place.

But the service responsibility is also a matter of maintaining communication with the primary company as to new territories, new products, changes of philosophy, personnel and so on. Sometimes the primary company may need help with accounting or data processing techniques or in evaluating claims procedures or the adequacy of claims reserves. In many such instances the intermediary refers the company to a specialty firm; in some cases the intermediary's own staff may provide the answers. Only by keeping current with the company's progress can an intermediary avert potential problems and fine tune or drastically change the reinsurance program to suit the company's needs.

# Loss Development

By Joseph W. Levin
Vice President and Actuary, Employers Reinsurance Corporation

FOR MOST PROPERTY AND CASUALTY INSUR-
ANCE companies, both primary insurers and reinsurers, the largest entry on the liabilities side of the
balance sheet is for loss and loss expense reserves.
Determining what these reserves should be is a function
of the company's claims and actuarial departments.

Two major factors in the calculation or valuation process are the
time it takes for all details of any given loss to emerge and accounting
for "incurred but not reported" (IBNR) insured losses. The difference
between the initial estimated amount of reported losses and the
estimated amount at a later date, or paid out in final settlement, is
known as "loss development." This chapter will discuss loss
development from the viewpoint of a reinsurer in terms of:

1. Claims department functions;
2. Actuarial department functions;
3. Reinsurance Association of America Loss Development Study;
   and
4. A comparison of primary insurer and reinsurer loss development
   patterns.

## CLAIMS DEPARTMENT FUNCTION

In both primary insurance and reinsurance companies the primary
functions of a claims department are to reserve judiciously and

**37**

prudently, to distribute analyses of loss reserves and claims, to issue funds to claimants at a fair settlement cost and to help protect the assets of the insurance entity.

However, there are several important differences between the claims departments of primary companies and those of reinsurers. In a primary company, the claims department handles the administration of all the claims submitted by the company's policyholders in many different lines of the insurance business. Small companies without a claims department generally contract for such services from a professional claims handling organization. In either case, the claims handling process includes payment of claims, the accumulation of statistics and the reporting of such information. The activities in the claims department of a reinsurer are somewhat different. In settling claims, the reinsurer deals with the primary insurer, not the original policyholder. In addition, it does not get involved with all the individual claims processed by the primary company, only with claims of a serious nature or of a high value, claims of fairly low frequency. The reinsurer's claims department also is responsible for providing technical support. In legal areas, for example, it may provide information of a general nature about judicial proceedings and the individuals involved, and assistance in the selection of experienced and competent counsel to aid, when necessary, in the legal defense of claims.

The claims department in both primary and reinsurance companies usually is responsible for the reporting of claims. The format of such reporting varies by product line and type of contract. One form of reporting is a monthly account that lists individual claims (especially for excess-of-loss reinsurance contracts). Included are data essential for annual statement reporting, such as the accident date, line of business, location, and the amount of payments, expenses and outstanding losses.

Claims under pro rata treaties tend to be reported in summary form, other than for catastrophe claims. Serious claims or catastrophes are generally reported immediately, as prompt action is often needed to provide proper claims control. In such cases, the reinsurer may be able to recover losses on its retrocession contracts. (Retrocession is a transaction through which a reinsurer cedes reinsurance to another reinsurer.)

Many reinsurers require reporting of excess-of-loss claims at a percentage of retention—such as 50 percent. When a primary company has a retention of $100,000, for example, all claims of $50,000 or greater should be reported. This gives the reinsurer, upon audit, the opportunity to consider whether any of these claims is likely to exceed the retention and therefore to involve reinsurance coverages.

It is a common practice among reinsurers to audit a ceding company's claims files. The claims audit is carried out on a periodic basis, usually semiannually or annually, as a cooperative effort between the primary company and reinsurer. The major objectives of the audit are:

1. To understand the philosophy, procedure, and attitudes of the ceding company's claims department and management;
2. To allow the reinsurer's underwriters to gain insight into the risks being accepted; and
3. To provide assistance in the handling of difficult or unusual cases.

The benefits of such audits accrue to both parties. The audit serves as a check and balance to the ceding company's own claims system and, in addition, it gives the reinsurer the opportunity to help the primary insurer with its reporting procedures and to reduce the need for IBNR reserves.

One of the greatest problems the reinsurer faces is failure on the part of the ceding company to report claims likely to involve the reinsurer. The main cause of this problem, in most cases, is a combination of faulty ceding company claims supervision, under-reserving (underestimating the ultimate loss amount), and neglecting basic treaty provisions. In addition, claims sometimes are not reported when injuries are serious but long-term disability appears to be remote.

IBNR reserves for a reinsurer (as opposed to a primary company) may be defined as the sum of (1) a provision for losses that have not been reported by the primary insurer to the reinsurer at a "valuation" point in time, and (2) a provision to adjust those claims that have been reported by the primary company but have been under-reserved (underestimated) because of lack of information or for some other reason. The sum of IBNR and case-basis (reported) reserves appears on the balance sheet of the annual statement under "liabilities for losses and loss adjustment expense."

After the audit has been carried out, the overall results are shared with the primary company's claims manager. The audit's ultimate purpose is to summarize briefly the amount by which reinsured claims cases should be changed, opened or closed.

Perhaps the most important role of the reinsurer's claims department is to establish reserves for losses. The reserving phase can be thought of as the integration of the reporting, investigation, research and underwriting processes. The methods and procedures vary by line and form of coverage. Usually no special attention is given to pro rata reinsurance since the gross loss is used as the basis for the reinsurer's portion of liability.

In calculating reserves, treaty excess-of-loss casualty coverages offer the greatest challenge to claims examiners. There is no set rule for determining correct reserves. In liability cases, the reinsurer will generally follow the reserve practices of the ceding company. However, if in the judgment of the examiner the primary company's reserve is too high or too low, an adjustment is made.

## ACTUARIAL DEPARTMENT FUNCTION

The actuary usually determines the amount of IBNR reserves. This is done by a process of estimation, according to historic loss development patterns. Accepted actuarial methods then are applied to trend, adjust or otherwise modify such data so that ultimate loss costs by line and by accident-year-of-business can be estimated.

Reported losses are defined as the sum of the valuation of reported unpaid losses at various points of time and the accumulation of paid claims to that point in time. These data usually are set out in a triangular array (see Exhibit A). Since the main objective of actuaries is to determine ultimate costs of each line of business by accident year, they must necessarily rely on various projection methods, using known data to project the future development path of those data. At any point in time the difference between ultimate loss costs and the reported losses to that point is considered IBNR. (This terminology is usual but is somewhat misleading. Differences between reported losses and ultimate loss costs will arise because of incorrect estimation, in addition to non-reported losses.)

It is the actuary's role to carry out studies on these data on a regular basis, either monthly or quarterly or at least annually. The actuary's report on the amount of reserves needed is transmitted to company management and eventually to the company's accounting department for completion of the required statutory or public reports. For some reinsurers the amount of IBNR is greater than reported reserves. This is especially true of companies writing a fairly high proportion of casualty excess-of-loss reinsurance.

---

## Exhibit A
### Reported Losses by Year of Accident for General Liability (Excluding Asbestos)

*Basic Data Triangle (000 omitted)*

**Evaluation Point (Measured in Years)**

**Accident**

| Year | Year 1 | Year 2 | Year 3 | Year 4 | Year 5 |
|------|--------|--------|--------|--------|--------|
| 1982 | $42,409 | $ 95,542 | $176,673 | $237,057 | $294,677 |
| 1983 | 31,623 | 92,069 | 174,755 | 241,564 | |
| 1984 | 43,950 | 136,242 | 243,534 | | |
| 1985 | 46,950 | 139,887 | | | |
| 1986 | 53,129 | | | | |

EXPLANATORY NOTES:

This table shows estimates of reported losses associated with accidents that occurred in a particular year. These loss estimates change from year to year as more information becomes known. In 1982, for example, losses for accidents occurring in 1982 were estimated to be $42,409,000. The following year (year 2, i.e., 1983) loss estimates for accidents that occurred in 1982 were changed to $95,542,000, a 125 percent increase over the original amount. The substantial difference between these two amounts, and similar year-to-year changes in the so-called "early years" (those immediately following the accident year), are largely due to IBNR losses. Basic data triangles may be established for any number of years.

## REINSURANCE ASSOCIATION OF AMERICA LOSS DEVELOPMENT STUDY

Within the several lines of business covered by reinsurance, none are characterized by the slow emergence of claims to a greater degree than casualty excess-of-loss reinsurance. In casualty excess-of-loss reinsurance accidents may be reported to the reinsurer at the time of the loss or many years later. Medical malpractice claims are particularly slow to emerge: The symptoms of the negligence that will ultimately lead a patient to file a claim may not be apparent for months or years—in a case of infant mental retardation caused by improper delivery, for example. More time may elapse before the symptoms are properly diagnosed and related to the treatment that the patient received. In addition, in an excess-of-loss agreement, the primary insurer may wait until the retention level is breached before notifying the reinsurer of the claim.

To aid in the understanding and measurement of such emergence, in terms useful for loss reserving, the Reinsurance Association of America (RAA) produces, on a biennial basis, a compilation of loss reserve development patterns. These patterns are compiled for lines of business in which emergence patterns traditionally are slower for reinsurance than for primary coverages. Specifically, the RAA study deals with automobile liability, general liability, workers' compensation and medical malpractice. It should be reemphasized that most of this business is written on an excess-of-loss basis.

The purpose of this compilation is to heighten awareness of loss development patterns among people involved in casualty excess-of-loss reinsurance or high deductible umbrella insurance. (Umbrella insurance is a form of protection against losses in excess of the amount covered by other liability policies.) Acquiring this awareness is the first and most important step toward achieving adequate loss reserve levels.

The RAA study helps measure and define the shape of loss development patterns, sometimes referred to as the "tail." The length of the tail depends on the line of business and in many cases it varies also by company. Loss development patterns or emergence curves have been developed from the RAA compilations using actuarial techniques to project loss development data to ultimate loss costs. The

RAA study uses one of the more frequently used projection methods to estimate the values plotted in the accompanying graphs.

Exhibit B shows the emergence curve for automobile liability, general liability, medical malpractice and workers' compensation. Automobile liability is seen to be the fastest "developing" line of insurance, meaning that it has a relatively shorter tail. At the end of a given accident year, 26 percent of ultimate auto liability claims dollars is expected to be reported to the reinsurer; by the end of the third year this value is expected to climb to 69 percent and by the fifth year more than 80 percent of ultimate claims costs is expected to be reported to the reinsurer.

Medical malpractice is very slow to develop. At the one-, two- or four-year development marks, 1 percent, 4 percent and 18 percent of ultimate costs are expected to be reported. Only 38 percent is expected by the eighth year and development is gradual thereafter.

General liability is also very slow to develop. The first-, second- and fourth-year development values are 5 percent, 15 percent and 36 percent, respectively. At the eighth year about 62 percent of ultimate claims are expected to be reported. The remainder is reported slowly, sometimes over as long a period as two decades.

Since the National Association of Insurance Commissioners did not require separate reporting of medical malpractice until recent years, limited data are available for that line. Due to the relatively short time that these data have been available, it was necessary to extrapolate emergence curves to ultimate levels for these lines.

However, in analyzing loss development, other factors must be considered in addition to historical emergence patterns. Recently, contributing RAA companies have observed a general lengthening of loss development patterns—an elongation of the tail. It appears that, almost without exception, each year's additional information has proved that previously indicated patterns underestimated ultimate costs. The 1989 RAA Study, which will be available in mid 1989, is not expected to show any dramatic change in this pattern.

To demonstrate this, the RAA compared emergence curves for the three lines, based on the data available at the end of years 1978, 1982 and 1986. These emergence curves were drawn using the same methodology discussed above, but on data available through the year

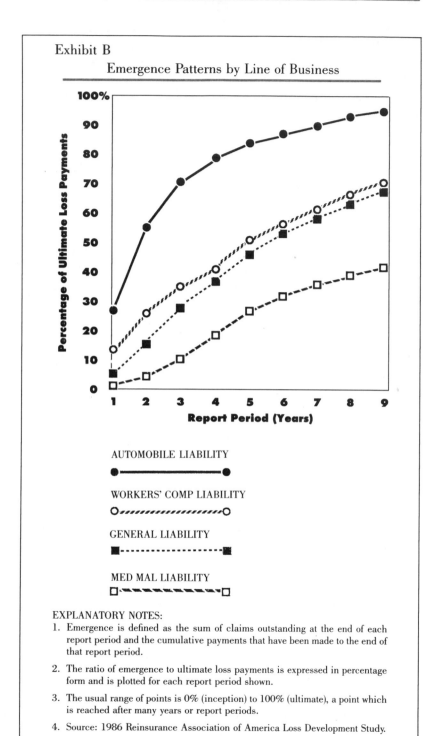

Exhibit B

Emergence Patterns by Line of Business

AUTOMOBILE LIABILITY

WORKERS' COMP LIABILITY

GENERAL LIABILITY

MED MAL LIABILITY

EXPLANATORY NOTES:

1. Emergence is defined as the sum of claims outstanding at the end of each report period and the cumulative payments that have been made to the end of that report period.

2. The ratio of emergence to ultimate loss payments is expressed in percentage form and is plotted for each report period shown.

3. The usual range of points is 0% (inception) to 100% (ultimate), a point which is reached after many years or report periods.

4. Source: 1986 Reinsurance Association of America Loss Development Study.

end indicated. An example of the trend for automobile liability can be seen in Exhibit C-1. At the end of the second year of development, the 1978 data suggested that 68 percent of ultimate claims would be reported. The corresponding data for 1982 and 1986 show a progressively slower emergence of claim costs—60 percent and 54 percent, respectively. Similar phenomena can be found for the other lines of business which are shown in Exhibits C-2, C-3 and C-4.

Factors contributing to these changing patterns are:

1. In the area of automobile liability, the inflationary effects on settlements of rising costs for the unlimited medical benefits provided in some states that have no-fault automobile insurance, changes in guest statutes (laws defining the driver's liability for other non-paying occupants in the event of an accident) and changes in social attitudes.

2. Inflationary effects similar to those shown for automobile liability also can be seen in general liability. These would include the change from contributory to comparative negligence in most states, "social" inflation and medical expense inflation. Contributory and comparative negligence are legal concepts which affect the amount of damages people injured in accidents receive. Under the comparative negligence rule, the settlement amount is reduced in proportion to the injured person's negligent actions or responsibility for causing the accident. In the six states and the District of Columbia where the contributory negligence rule applies, if the injured person is in any way responsible for the accident, compensation for the injury is denied. Social inflation means increased public awareness of high awards and the propensity to litigate in almost all questionable cases. Changes in the mix of business may also be influencing development patterns since products liability, which has an extremely long tail, is included in general liability.

3. Loss experience in workers' compensation is related both to the cost of medical care and to providing compensation for loss. Such compensation would include periodic pension-type payments for long-term disabilities or, in the case of death, payments to a survivor. Affecting development in this line is the increasing emergence of occupational disease claims (primarily those related to the use of asbestos), increased longevity and a reduced rate of

survivor remarriage (survivor benefits in most states are eliminated upon remarriage). In addition, loss development patterns have been affected by a liberalization trend on the part of authorities administering the workers' compensation laws and benefits.

4. In the area of medical malpractice, slow emergence is tied to the manifestation of symptoms. For example, in the case of newborn infants, lack of oxygen during the first minutes of delivery may not become apparent until measurable mental retardation can be observed years later. An additional factor pushing up costs is the high level of expectation applied to a science that is still not capable of producing completely predictable results. Failure to achieve expected results leads to the filing of lawsuits. The increased size of awards, including punitive damages, also is a factor in changing development or emergence patterns.

This list of contributing factors, while not exhaustive, does provide a partial explanation of the trends observed. The trends of the 1970s are now obvious, but only with the benefit of hindsight. The implications for the remaining portion of the 1980s and for the 1990s are uncertain. Reserving for latent injury cases, in particular asbestos-related diseases and black lung diseases, will continue to be challenging. It seems likely that there will be further lengthening of loss development patterns.

Since the data in the RAA study were obtained from a diverse industry, the study comes with caveats:

1. The data consist of losses in excess of underlying retentions. Such retentions vary from company to company and over time. Ideally, excess-of-loss experience would be studied separately for various retention/limit combinations or ranges thereof. Future RAA compilations contemplate this classification.

2. Most companies are reporting net of their reinsurance or retrocession. Retrocession retentions have also been increasing over time and will vary from reinsurer to reinsurer.

3. Geographic marketing and legal jurisdictions vary widely.

4. Underwriting rules vary from company to company.

5. Loss development patterns consist of actual late reporting, and adjustment of known reserves for incorrect initial estimates (underestimates). For reinsurers, the greatest portion of loss development comes from true late reporting.

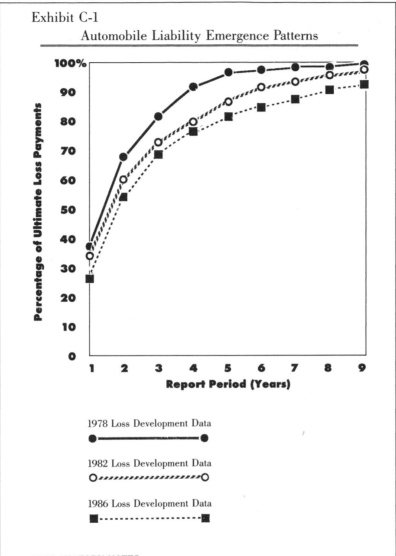

Exhibit C-1

Automobile Liability Emergence Patterns

1978 Loss Development Data

1982 Loss Development Data

1986 Loss Development Data

EXPLANATORY NOTES:
1. Emergence is defined as the sum of claims outstanding at the end of each report period and the cumulative payments that have been made to the end of that report period.

2. The ratio of emergence to ultimate loss payments is expressed in percentage form and is plotted for each report period shown.

3. The three separate lines are emergence patterns based on data available as of the year ending 1978, 1982 and 1986, respectively.

4. Source: 1986 Reinsurance Association of America Loss Development Study.

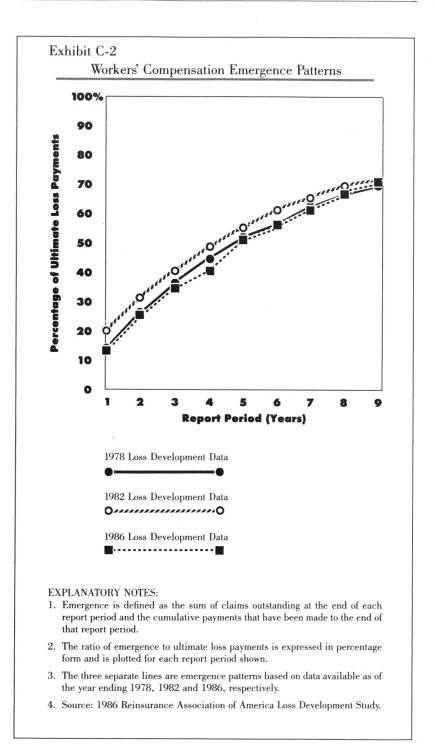

Exhibit C-2

Workers' Compensation Emergence Patterns

1978 Loss Development Data

1982 Loss Development Data

1986 Loss Development Data

EXPLANATORY NOTES:
1. Emergence is defined as the sum of claims outstanding at the end of each report period and the cumulative payments that have been made to the end of that report period.
2. The ratio of emergence to ultimate loss payments is expressed in percentage form and is plotted for each report period shown.
3. The three separate lines are emergence patterns based on data available as of the year ending 1978, 1982 and 1986, respectively.
4. Source: 1986 Reinsurance Association of America Loss Development Study.

Exhibit C-3
General Liability (Excluding Asbestos) Emergence Patterns

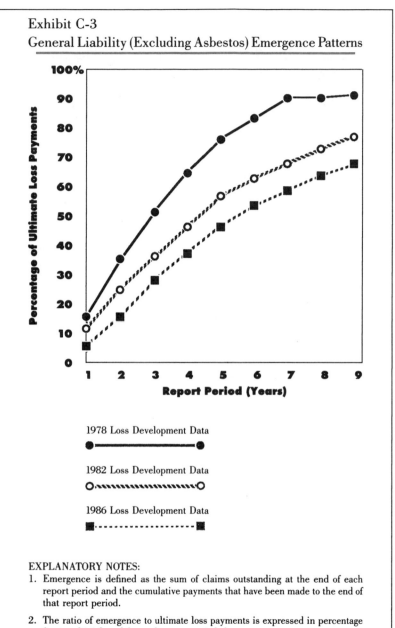

1978 Loss Development Data

1982 Loss Development Data

1986 Loss Development Data

EXPLANATORY NOTES:
1. Emergence is defined as the sum of claims outstanding at the end of each report period and the cumulative payments that have been made to the end of that report period.

2. The ratio of emergence to ultimate loss payments is expressed in percentage form and is plotted for each report period shown.

3. The three separate lines are emergence patterns based on data available as of the year ending 1978, 1982 and 1986, respectively.

4. Source: 1986 Reinsurance Association of America Loss Development Study.

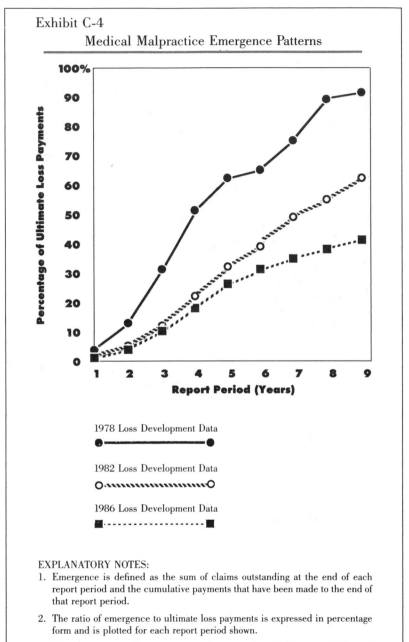

Exhibit C-4

Medical Malpractice Emergence Patterns

*Percentage of Ultimate Loss Payments* (y-axis)

*Report Period (Years)* (x-axis)

1978 Loss Development Data

1982 Loss Development Data

1986 Loss Development Data

EXPLANATORY NOTES:

1. Emergence is defined as the sum of claims outstanding at the end of each report period and the cumulative payments that have been made to the end of that report period.

2. The ratio of emergence to ultimate loss payments is expressed in percentage form and is plotted for each report period shown.

3. The three separate lines are emergence patterns based on data available as of the year ending 1978, 1982 and 1986, respectively.

4. Source: 1986 Reinsurance Association of America Loss Development Study.

6. Alternate coverage techniques, such as indexing, can cause distortions in developments. Indexing is a concept which, in theory, spreads the cost of inflation equitably between the primary company and the reinsurer. This is accomplished by application of an index factor to the retention of the primary company. This retention will rise as the selected index rises. The effect of this, however, is that reinsurer involvement is deferred to higher levels of coverage but it also may leverage the reinsurer's involvement. This leverage effect is discussed later in this chapter.

If the RAA loss development data are to be used to project ultimate losses for an individual company, especially in the earlier years of development, extreme caution should be exercised. Variance in "immature" years is large. Early reported data can be volatile and lead to incorrect conclusions if heavily relied upon. The RAA study discusses individual company loss development variations.

In summary, the RAA study, which is based on the only known compilation of casualty excess-of-loss reinsurance loss reserve development data, is intended to make the reader aware of loss development patterns and their variations by line of business. In addition, it highlights the trends by line toward longer tails. Although accompanied by necessary caveats, the study can and should be used in individual company loss reserve analysis as a guide to average expected emergence of losses. Loss reserve adequacy, as mentioned before, is the primary objective of most insurance company actuaries and their management. Generally, in measuring loss reserve adequacy, it is up to loss reserve specialists in each company to differentiate between their company's characteristics and those of the industry average in measuring the company's loss reserve adequacy. Loss reserve adequacy, as mentioned before, is the primary objective of most insurance company actuaries and their management.

## COMPARISON OF PRIMARY AND REINSURANCE LOSS DEVELOPMENT PATTERNS

In the prior section, loss development patterns were compared by line of business. The comparison showed how loss development patterns vary from one line of business to another. But they also vary substantially between the two segments of the insurance industry—reinsurers and primary insurers. The major reason for this difference is the delay in reporting claims to reinsurers, despite steps taken to accelerate such reporting. The problem of delay is most active in excess-of-loss reinsurance for casualty business.

The four graphs in Exhibits D, E, F and G show the relative emergence patterns for primary companies and reinsurers. Emergence means cumulative paid and unpaid reserves at various points in time of development. Emergence does not include IBNR losses. The four graphs shown represent the typical patterns of emergence of claims for a primary company and a reinsurer, for automobile liability, workers' compensation, general liability and medical malpractice. The plots are incurred losses (exclusive of estimates of IBNR) as a percentage of ultimate liability at annual valuation dates. In the case of automobile liability, at the end of an accident year the primary insurer is aware of about 80 percent of its ultimate liability whereas the reinsurer knows of only 26 percent of its liability. At the end of three years the primary insurer knows of approximately 98 percent, but the reinsurer knows of only 69 percent.

In the general liability line of insurance the disparity is more pronounced. The corresponding data for one- and three-year development patterns are 37 percent for the primary insurer versus 4 percent for the reinsurer for the first year, and 80 percent versus 23 percent for the third year of development. At the end of seven years the reinsurer usually knows of only 49 percent of its ultimate liability.

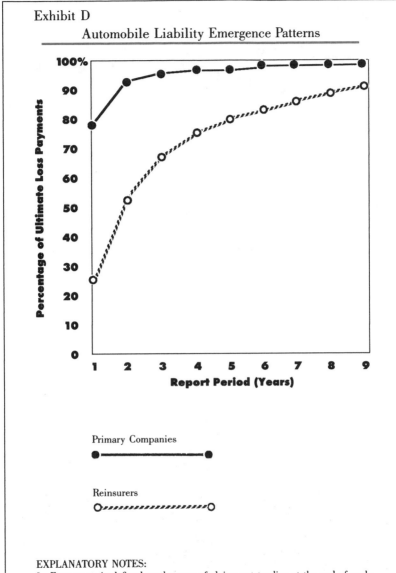

Exhibit D

Automobile Liability Emergence Patterns

Primary Companies

Reinsurers

EXPLANATORY NOTES:
1. Emergence is defined as the sum of claims outstanding at the end of each report period and the cumulative payments that have been made to the end of that report period.

2. The ratio of emergence to ultimate loss payments is expressed in percentage form and is plotted for each report period shown.

3. Sources: (a) 1986 Reinsurance Association of America Loss Development Study.
   (b) Annual statements of selected primary insurance companies.

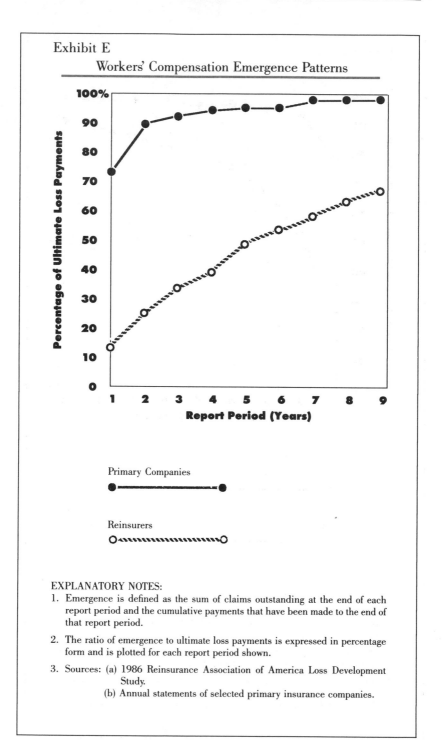

Exhibit E

Workers' Compensation Emergence Patterns

Primary Companies

Reinsurers

EXPLANATORY NOTES:

1. Emergence is defined as the sum of claims outstanding at the end of each report period and the cumulative payments that have been made to the end of that report period.

2. The ratio of emergence to ultimate loss payments is expressed in percentage form and is plotted for each report period shown.

3. Sources: (a) 1986 Reinsurance Association of America Loss Development Study.
    (b) Annual statements of selected primary insurance companies.

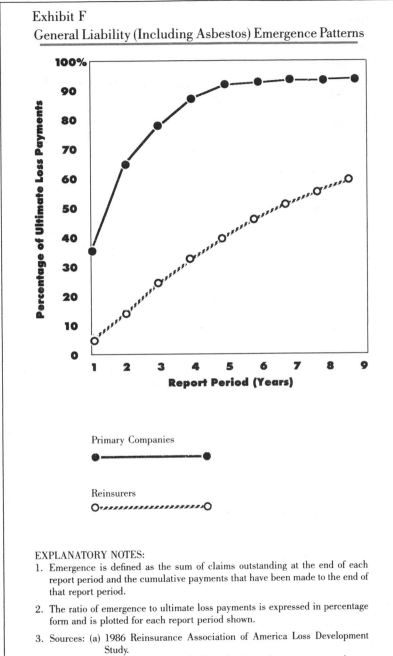

### Exhibit F
### General Liability (Including Asbestos) Emergence Patterns

Primary Companies

Reinsurers

EXPLANATORY NOTES:
1. Emergence is defined as the sum of claims outstanding at the end of each report period and the cumulative payments that have been made to the end of that report period.

2. The ratio of emergence to ultimate loss payments is expressed in percentage form and is plotted for each report period shown.

3. Sources: (a) 1986 Reinsurance Association of America Loss Development Study.
   (b) Annual statements of selected primary insurance companies.

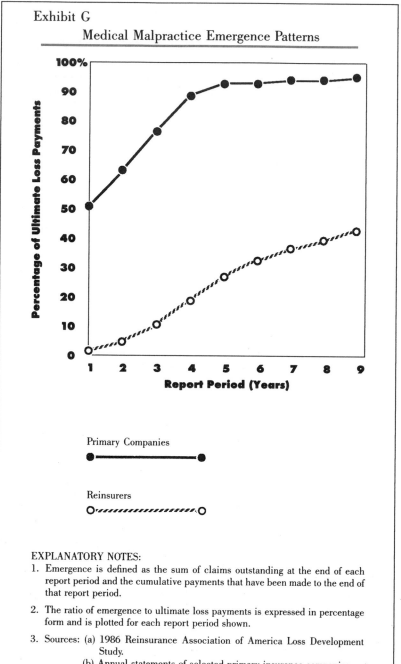

Exhibit G

Medical Malpractice Emergence Patterns

*Percentage of Ultimate Loss Payments* (y-axis)

*Report Period (Years)* (x-axis)

Primary Companies

Reinsurers

EXPLANATORY NOTES:

1. Emergence is defined as the sum of claims outstanding at the end of each report period and the cumulative payments that have been made to the end of that report period.

2. The ratio of emergence to ultimate loss payments is expressed in percentage form and is plotted for each report period shown.

3. Sources: (a) 1986 Reinsurance Association of America Loss Development Study.
   (b) Annual statements of selected primary insurance companies.

Workers' compensation shows a pattern similar to general liability. The primary company learns of most of its ultimate liability within three years while after 10 years only 65 percent of reinsurers' ultimate loss amounts are reported.

Inflation, to a certain degree, is a factor in the elongation of the emergence pattern. Mention was made earlier of the leverage effect of inflation in excess-of-loss reinsurance. The following example highlights the effect of inflation on the reinsurer in excess-of-loss casualty contracts. Assume a contract has a $50,000 retention per individual policy and that, without inflation, there are 36 claims incurred by the primary company, as follows:

## The Effect of Inflation on Excess-of-Loss Casualty Contracts

Diagram I

| # of Claims Ceded | Amount of Each Loss | Total Loss Amount | Amount of Loss Retained | Amount of Loss |
|---|---|---|---|---|
| 11 | $ 15,000 | $   165,000 | $   165,000 | $       0 |
| 9 | 25,000 | 225,000 | 225,000 | 0 |
| 7 | 35,000 | 245,000 | 245,000 | 0 |
| 5 | 48,000 | 240,000 | 240,000 | 0 |
| 3 | 55,000 | 165,000 | 150,000 | 15,000 |
| 1 | 65,000 | 65,000 | 50,000 | 15,000 |
| 36 | | $ 1,105,000 | $ 1,075,000 | $30,000 |

Now assume a 10 percent rate of inflation overall. The distribution of losses would then be as follows:

Diagram II

| # of Claims Ceded | Amount of Each Loss | Total Loss Amount | Amount of Loss Retained | Amount of Loss |
|---|---|---|---|---|
| 11 | $ 16,500 | $    181,500 | $    181,500 | $    0 |
| 9 | 27,500 | 247,500 | 247,500 | 0 |
| 7 | 38,500 | 269,500 | 269,500 | 0 |
| 5 | 52,800 | 264,000 | 250,000 | 14,000 |
| 3 | 60,500 | 181,500 | 150,000 | 31,500 |
| 1 | 71,500 | 71,500 | 50,000 | 21,500 |
| 36 | | $ 1,215,500 | $ 1,148,500 | $ 67,000 |

Without inflation (Diagram I) four claims totaling $30,000 were ceded to the reinsurer. With inflation (Diagram II) nine claims totaling $67,000 were ceded. The impact of a 10 percent inflation factor caused the amount of each loss to increase. For example, the five claims of $48,000 each (Diagram I) increased to $52,800 (Diagram II) or $2,800 above the retention of $50,000 per policy, bringing the amount ceded to the reinsurer to $14,000. As a result, the primary company's total amount of retained losses increased by 7 percent from $1,075,000 to $1,148,500, but the reinsurer's portion of losses increased by 123 percent from $30,000 to $67,000. Not only are more claims involved but the average amount of claims increased more dramatically for reinsurers.

# CHAPTER 5

# Changes in the Reinsurance Environment

By Gerald F. Fisher
Vice President and Special Counsel,
North American Reinsurance Corporation

## INTRODUCTION

O ne of the few certainties in the reinsurance environment over the past decade has been the certainty of change. New challenges have arisen almost continuously in an unprecedented and extremely difficult environment. Risk exposures have increased, capital structures have become more fragile and competition in the reinsurance market has become increasingly intense. In addition, external factors, such as taxation and regulation, are exerting greater influence on company decision-making and operations.

These and many other changes have brought about fundamental shifts in management philosophy and in relationships with ceding companies, the reinsurer's clients.

The following sections of this chapter will discuss in greater detail some of the factors that caused these changes and explore the impact that they have had upon reinsurers.

## INCREASED RISK EXPOSURE

In many respects, the reinsurance industry and the primary insurance industry face similar problems. Both have experienced an increase in risk exposures, a long-term trend that shows no sign of abating and that affects tort liability as well as property insurance coverages. This increase can be seen in the volume of civil litigation, in the size of average jury awards, and in both the number and dollar amount of insurance company claim payments.

Many factors have contributed to this growth, among them recent developments in the legal environment in the United States. As mentioned in other sections of this monograph, changes in legal doctrine over the last few decades have expanded liability which, in turn, has dramatically increased insurance liability claims. For example, in product liability cases, a negligence standard of liability has been replaced with a standard of strict liability. To receive damages, all the plaintiff need prove is that the product defect caused the injury. The presence or absence of negligence on the part of the plaintiff is irrelevant. In some states, the contributory negligence rule which bars compensation if there was any negligence on the part of the plaintiff has given way to the concept of comparative negligence which permits plaintiffs to recover according to their degree of fault in the accident. Another factor pushing up claim payments in tort cases has been the application of the rule of joint and several liability under which any defendant found to have contributed in any way to the injury may be held liable for the entire amount of damages if that defendant is the only solvent defendant. This change has caused plaintiffs' attorneys to sue all conceivable parties and even parties unknown at the time the suit is filed (to preserve all possible future claims and avoid charges of malpractice later on), thus increasing in geometric progression the scale, expense and procedural complexity of virtually all tort litigation.

Some of these legal developments have grown out of the need to assess liability for injuries arising from evolving technologies and the goods produced through use of these technologies. Advances in transportation and communication have promoted the globalization of industries, creating a worldwide market for new products, many of which pose dangers to their users that are currently unknown, or not effectively communicated. In addition, many manufacturing processes and raw materials extraction and processing operations generate wastes that ultimately may prove dangerous to human beings, animals and other forms of life.

Unfortunately, these dangers sometimes are not fully understood until many years or decades after the products have been put to general use. And even more distressing, some manufacturers, motivated by the desire for continued profits, have continued to make certain products despite data internally communicated to management suggesting possible health risks. The history of asbestos is the most notorious example of this disregard for safety, but it is by no means unique.

Asbestos was widely used as a building material and in many industrial applications, such as automobile brake linings. Although we now recognize, with hindsight, that there were signs that asbestos could cause disease, the problem was not widely acknowledged until the 1960s. The story of hazardous wastes has been similar.

The injuries caused by asbestos and other toxic substances—so called toxic torts—have given rise to complex and often costly lawsuits. These, in turn, have prompted companies being sued to attempt to reconstruct their insurance policies over a period of many years to determine whether they have insurance coverage for the injuries and property damage for which they might be liable. Injuries and property damage caused by environmental pollution are most commonly addressed by liability insurance, but this exposure also may be covered by the debris cleanup provisions of property insurance policies. The by-products of fires and explosions release toxic substances into the environment and the cost of neutralizing or removing these wastes, often covered by property insurance, has been a subject of major concern.

In addition to the highly publicized dangers to public health and safety arising from the use of new materials and new technologies, other more mundane developments, such as the expansion of municipal liability, have affected the primary insurance industry, and, consequently, the reinsurance industry as well. Coverage for municipal liability has been difficult to obtain in recent years due to a combination of several factors, including the erosion of traditional doctrines of governmental immunity from tort liability and the expansion of municipal services into areas where the doctrine of governmental immunity would not apply.

Along with the expansion and changes in the types of liability which insurance has been called upon to address, there has been another significant development: an increase in the amount of time between the period for which an insurance policy is issued and the period in which claims are reported, commonly referred to as the long liability tail. Since insurance and reinsurance must be priced long before the cost is known, this ever-widening time gap makes the pricing of liability insurance and reinsurance extremely difficult.

Another aspect of the growth of risk exposure is the increased amount of values to be insured, a trend that is evident to anyone in the market for a house or a new car. But the escalation in values is not confined to personal items. Businesses are experiencing a similar phenomenon. An extreme example is the cost of the Piper Alpha oil drilling platform, which was destroyed in a storm in the North Sea. At the time of this writing, loss of this oil rig is expected to cost insurers and reinsurers more than $1.4 billion.

With the rise in values has come a greater geographic concentration of values. The population of the United States has been drifting toward the east and west coasts for many years and, as a result, there has been extensive development of coastal areas for both residential and commercial purposes. This growth has taken place despite the fact that these areas are exposed to natural disasters, in the form of hurricanes on the Atlantic and Gulf coasts, and earthquakes in regions near the Pacific coast. Seismologists now warn that a major earthquake is also likely to shake the East coast within the next two decades.

Beyond the expansion of tort liability and the increase in the amounts and concentrations of values to be insured, both the insurance and reinsurance industries have had to face a legal system which appears to see insurance companies as a "deep pocket"—a way of funding any and all claims for damages brought before the courts. Whether or not this perception is accurate depends on one's analysis and interpretation of the mass of conflicting information on the subject. Each observer tends to see the data through the filter of his or her own prejudices and preconceptions.

A more fundamental problem for the insurance industry lies in the legal system's lack of predictability. American legal scholars and professionals view the ability of the courts to fashion new remedies, and indeed to create new laws, as one of the glories of our common law system. Consider for example, the 1916 landmark case of MacPherson vs. Buick Motor Co. When a lower court held that the owner of an automobile could not sue the manufacturer of that automobile for a defect which caused an accident, because there was no privity of contract (legal relationship) between the owner and the manufacturer, the Court of Appeals of the State of New York simply abolished the defense of privity of contract for manufactured products. As long as the courts have the power to create and abolish rules of law, whether they relate to privity of contract or contributory negligence or, more recently, the right to an abortion, the legal system will not have the degree of predictability which insurers and reinsurers once assumed it had. In retrospect, we can see that the legal system never had the degree of predictability that many believed it had, but it is only in recent years that insurers and reinsurers have begun to understand this. (In the meantime, the primary insurance industry is pressing forward with tort reform which, while it may mitigate the impact of some specific legal problems, will not change the system's fundamental and inherent characteristics.)

## IMPACT ON REINSURERS OF INCREASED RISK EXPOSURE

The growth in loss exposures faced by primary insurers has had a profound impact on reinsurers. Much of the increased risk in underwriting these exposures is being transferred to reinsurers as the result of basic changes in the reinsurance business itself. One such trend has been the enormous growth in facultative reinsurance.

Facultative reinsurance developed out of a practice common 20 years ago of making special "acceptances" to treaty reinsurance—taking out of the treaty or accepting specific policies to underwrite separately—and since then, it has grown to be a major segment of the reinsurance business. As is explained elsewhere in this monograph, facultative reinsurance is priced by the reinsurer on a risk-by-risk basis. The reinsurer's pricing is independent of the ceding company's pricing and there is no proportional sharing of the premiums and losses as there is in treaty reinsurance.

Another long-term trend is the shift in treaty reinsurance from pro rata to excess forms. Largely the result of a desire to reduce the constant flow of money between the ceding and assuming companies, excess-of-loss reinsurance gives the reinsurer fewer dollars for a potentially much greater risk exposure.

Over the years, the growth of facultative and excess-of-loss forms of reinsurance at the expense of treaty and pro-rata, has undermined the "partnership" nature of reinsurance so typical of reinsurance relationships in the past. A more recent development has been the increased size of ceding company retentions, mainly as a result of the hard market and the limited availability of reinsurance. This too has increased the underwriting risk to which reinsurers are exposed by reducing the portion of reinsurance in working layers (levels of coverage at which frequent but predictable small losses occur), thus leaving reinsurers with fewer dollars for larger amounts of potential risk exposure in the higher layers. In the uppermost layers, reinsurance premiums may be only a few dollars per thousand dollars of coverage. A single large claim, such as the asbestos liability claims or the North Sea Piper Alpha oil rig disaster, can consume many years' worth of premiums.

## RESPONSES TO INCREASED RISK EXPOSURE

Reinsurers have encouraged primary insurers to address those aspects of increased risk that are passed along to reinsurers, but the results so far have been limited. At a state level, the passage of tort reform measures has been uneven and at the federal level efforts to reform product liability law, even on a limited basis, so far have been unsuccessful.

Primary insurers' attempts to limit their liability through changes in contractual terms also have had mixed results. The claims-made policy, which some believed would facilitate the underwriting of long tail lines of business, has not been widely accepted either in the marketplace or by regulators and the courts. Reactions to other measures designed to reduce risk exposures, such as the adoption of additional coverage exclusions, have been similar. The best known of these, the pollution exclusion incorporated into commercial liability policies, has been dealt with harshly by both legislators and the courts.

The reinsurance industry has taken much the same approach to these problems. The result is reflected in reinsurance contract terms and in reinsurance program structures. Reinsurers have sought to limit their liabilities to ceding companies with long lists of exclusions, but these efforts, like those of the primary insurers, have met with limited acceptance. Likewise, the reinsurance equivalent of the claims-made policy, a "sunset" clause, under which all claims must be presented by the ceding company to the reinsurer within a limited period of time, typically four or five years, has encountered considerable resistance in the marketplace. The sunset clause is part of what is sometimes referred to as "non-traditional" or "finite risk" reinsurance, which includes various other limitations to protect the reinsurer. While non-traditional reinsurance has not been well received by the industry, it has not been totally rejected and does appear to be carving out a modest niche.

In the last several years, the initial (and most publicized) response to the problems reviewed above has been withdrawal from the business. In some cases the withdrawal has been involuntary as reinsurers, both domestic and foreign, have become insolvent. The most spectacular insolvency has been that of the Mission Insurance Group, which was heavily involved in the reinsurance business and is reported to be insolvent by hundreds of millions of dollars. (However, most reinsurers have *not* become insolvent and indeed many of them, as a result of the turnaround in rates that began in 1984, are in good financial condition.) Both before and after the cycle turned, many reinsurers withdrew from specific segments of the market. They cut back operations to levels which their management believed they could effectively control, or they simply withdrew from those segments of the reinsurance business that appeared to offer an inadequate return for the capital and management time invested in them. One notable example of withdrawal from the market was the sale by General Reinsurance Corporation of its life reinsurance affiliate so that it could concentrate on its highly successful property and casualty reinsurance business.

Primary insurers also have withdrawn from segments of the primary market, raising concerns about availability. These concerns have been communicated to lawmakers in testimony before legislative committees and in regulatory hearings. In the past, availability problems typically were addressed by the creation of residual market mechanisms, such as automobile assigned risk plans and coastal windstorm pools. However, more recent developments in the marketplace—the withdrawal from municipal liability insurance by primary insurers, for example—have been approached differently. The preferred solution has been to set up organizations of various kinds, specialty insurance companies, that specialize in insuring a particular type of risk. While these organizations—captives, risk retention groups and other risk-sharing mechanisms—compete with primary insurers and are taking a substantial volume of business away from them, they often turn to reinsurers in the traditional marketplace for reinsurance coverage. Since these specialty insurers are relatively small, they are likely to buy more reinsurance than a larger primary company writing the same underlying risks. Thus if a reinsurer has the skills to underwrite the type of business involved, the displacement of risk exposure from the primary insurers to the specialty insurers represents an opportunity.

## LESS ROOM FOR ERROR

The reinsurance industry has been placed in the public spotlight as a result of the decision of the attorneys general of 20 states to charge major insurers and reinsurers with violation of antitrust laws. Although reinsurers, like insurers, are exempt from the general application of the federal and state antitrust laws by the McCarran-Ferguson Act and specific provisions in the state insurance laws, the industry is not protected for acts of boycott, coercion, or intimidation. Specifically, the attorneys general have charged insurers and reinsurers with a boycott of municipal liability insurance. They also contend that withdrawal from a line of business is not protected by the McCarran-Ferguson Act. These charges exemplify another characteristic of the new environment in which the reinsurance business must operate. This is what might be called "the reduced margin for error." Regardless of the substance of the charges, it is clear that the reinsurance business is now subject to a far greater degree of scrutiny than it was in the past. Now that it is in the public spotlight, significant errors of judgment will be reviewed in the courts and analyzed extensively in the media. This is a profound change for a business which was once almost unknown outside the insurance industry.

While risk exposures have increased for insurers in general and for reinsurers, in particular, the resources to meet these increased risk exposures have diminished. The fragile nature of the capital structure, resulting from the high level of reinsurance recoverable relative to insurance industry surplus, is a dramatic example of the industry's reduced ability to meet increasing exposures. According to statistics from the Insurance Services Office, Inc., a large portion of the total surplus of the property/casualty insurance business is offset by reinsurance recoverables, which, as of December 31, 1986, totalled about 85 percent of statutory surplus. If recoverables from affiliates are excluded, the proportion was only about 57 percent, but for a dozen major property and casualty commercial lines insurers the percentage was much higher.

To the extent that that reinsurance is not recoverable, surplus does not exist. Similarly, the reinsurance industry has much of its surplus offset by retrocessions recoverable from other reinsurers. Again, this fragility of capital is illustrated by the number of reinsurers, both large and small, that have collapsed or shut down their operations in recent years. In addition, the closing of the insurance exchanges in New York and Florida demonstrate that alternative structures specially established to conduct reinsurance business are exposed to the same kind of problems as reinsurers organized in the usual corporate fashion.

## COMPETITION

Although capital weakness has reduced flexibility and the margin for error, competition among reinsurers remains strong. The surge of new entrants, which characterized the development of the reinsurance business in the 1960s and 1970s, has largely abated, but the capital base of companies now in the marketplace is substantial, and new capital is entering the business. In some cases—Center Re, based in New York, Bermuda and Barbados, is an example—capital has been raised in the domestic or international capital markets to fund new reinsurers. In the past, capital for reinsurance came from not only general investors, but also from large businesses seeking to expand the scope of their activities, including a major steel company, a major oil company, a major finance company and several large life insurance companies. While some have withdrawn from the reinsurance market in the wake of disastrous financial results, others have survived and can be expected to continue in business. The most recent entrants have been commercial banks, which are attempting to enter the insurance business at every level, from the marketing of personal lines insurance to the underwriting of primary insurance and reinsurance.

In addition to financial capital, human capital—reinsurance expertise—is also readily available. In the 1960s and the 1970s, new reinsurers were typically established by people recruited from the handful of existing reinsurers. By contrast, today there is a large pool of experienced individuals with specialized knowledge of various types of reinsurance which makes entry into the reinsurance business relatively easy. This ease of entry remains one of the most remarkable facets of the business. In the market turnaround which began in 1984, several new professional reinsurers were quickly organized when capital became available. Able people were readily recruited for these new enterprises and reinsurance brokers were quick to bring them business.

Reinsurance brokers are major players in the property and casualty reinsurance business, ensuring a high degree of competition. Traditionally, roughly three-quarters of the property and casualty reinsurance business, measured by premium volume, has been handled by brokers, leaving about one quarter to the direct-writing professional reinsurers. Brokers' share of the business dropped somewhat in the market turnaround that began in 1984, but this does not appear to have substantially diminished their role in the reinsurance marketplace. The resulting competition has pushed rates down more rapidly than many had expected. Whether this decline puts rates at a level commensurate with the risks being assumed, considering the efforts by both reinsurers and primary insurers to limit their exposure as discussed above, remains to be seen.

## FINANCIAL MARKETS

The reinsurance industry is not isolated from other sectors of the financial industry. Indeed, in recent years the lines that once separated various segments have become increasingly blurred. Thus, stresses in other sectors, such as the precipitous decline in stock market values in October 1987, have had an impact on the reinsurance business and also have reduced the room for error. Fortunately, the decline in the stock market appears to have had little direct impact on most reinsurers, but it has had significant indirect effects. For example, it has increased the difficulty of raising capital through selling stock. For the insurance and reinsurance business, however, a far more serious problem has been the volatility of interest rates over the past decade. The extremely high interest rates of the late 1970s and early 1980s was one of the factors that led insurers and reinsurers into "cash flow" underwriting which put greater emphasis on generating cash flow for investment purposes than traditional underwriting strategies. When interest rates declined, those who had espoused cash flow underwriting were left exposed to cash shortfalls because earnings on reserves were substantially lower than had been expected at the time the policies were written. This reinvestment risk can have a severe impact on investment earnings from long-tail reserves. And because reinsurer reserves typically have longer tails than primary insurer reserves, interest rate volatility has a greater effect on the financial results of reinsurers than primary insurers.

The problems faced by the banking industry, another segment of the mammoth financial services industry, also have had an impact on reinsurers. Banks and savings and loan associations in the United States have just been through the most financially devastating period since the early 1930s. The practical effect of the banking industry's troubles on the reinsurance business has been the imposition of capital adequacy requirements for letters of credit issued by banks. This has increased the price charged for these letters. The importance of letters of credit, which are widely used to support alien reinsurance, is discussed in greater detail later in this monograph. The financial pressures and strains affecting other financial sectors have contributed to efforts by all participants in the financial services industry to broaden the scope of their activities in the hope of expanding their earnings base or decreasing their business risks through diversification. The result is new competition in each financial services sector. This phenomenon has been fostered by the widespread anti-regulatory attitude advocated by leaders of both major political parties and implemented by both the Carter and Reagan administrations. This gradual erosion of the barriers separating the various specialties which make up the financial services industry has generated new competition and, through a domino effect, poses potential new threats to the solvency of the whole system. Another potential danger, inflation, has been relatively subdued in recent years. In the 1970s and early 1980s, inflation—both economic and social—had a severe impact on the reinsurance industry as it drove ever-increasing numbers of claims into higher layers of reinsurance. Reinsurers tried to meet the threat of inflation by indexing retentions and setting dollar limits in reinsurance treaties so that they would move up with the rise in prices, but these measures were not well accepted in the marketplace. While inflation appears to have abated, as of this writing, some observers see signs of rising inflation ahead.

## TAXATION

Another factor will also give the reinsurance industry less room for error: increased federal taxation as a result of changes brought about by the Tax Reform Act of 1986. For many years, federal income taxation of property and casualty insurance and reinsurance was very closely tied to statutory accounting. The conservative nature of statutory accounting resulted in what was perceived, by some critics, to be a substantial tax benefit for the insurance and reinsurance business. As a result of the 1986 income tax law changes, property and casualty reinsurers now must discount loss reserves for tax purposes, thereby anticipating the investment income that they will earn on investments held for their reserves. The scope of this change is beyond this discussion, but it is important to understand that it could have profound effects upon the way insurers and reinsurers conduct their business. This discounting provision is likely to lead to higher prices. It also may encourage the reinsurance of business generating long-tail reserves to move to jurisdictions outside the United States, where tax treatment is more favorable or where there is, at least, some congruity between taxation accounting and accounting for financial statement presentation.

## RISING EXPECTATIONS

Another challenge to the reinsurance industry, which is not accustomed to being in the spotlight, is what might be termed "rising expectations": the demands placed on the industry by virtually everyone who deals with it. These include regulators, professional people, legislators, attorneys general, ceding companies and ultimately the general public. Regulator concerns about reinsurance have escalated enormously over the course of the last decade because of the growing number and size of insolvencies. In the 1970s and even earlier, the National Association of Insurance Commissioners (NAIC) dealt with the subject of reinsurance on a sporadic basis. Since that time reinsurance has come to permeate many aspects of the commissioners' work. The NAIC's first concern is for the solvency of primary insurers, but because reinsurance recoverables represent such an important asset in the financial statements of primary insurers, commissioners must also pay careful attention to the value and collectibility of reinsurance as an asset.

This concern with issues relating to solvency, including accounting, reserving, investments and reinsurance, represents a fundamental shift from the commissioners' traditional concern with issues relating to rates, forms and sales and claims practices. Surprisingly, however, this has not led them to be more sympathetic to measures, such as the acceptance of the claims-made policy form, that attempt to address fundamental underwriting problems. Instead, the commissioners have sought more data on reinsurance and have issued substantive regulations affecting reinsurance transactions. Specifically, new schedules have been added to the annual financial statement to provide more information on loss development, including the loss development of assumed reinsurance. Also, the reinsurance recoverable schedules of the annual statement have been modified to show the extent of what potentially is uncollectible by requiring the "aging" of receivables. This is discussed in greater detail in another part of this monograph; see Chapter Eight. In addition to seeking more information, the commissioners are also seeking to have this information provided to them in ways that enable them to use it more quickly and easily, such as having annual statements filed in a computer-readable form so that each statement can be rapidly analyzed for signs of potential financial difficulty.

The commissioners have issued new regulations which impact substantively on reinsurance. The first such action was taken many years ago to reverse the result of the *Pink* case [*Fidelity & Deposit Company vs. Pink*, 32 U.S. 224 (1937)] and to require use of what is now considered the standard insolvency clause. This clause enables the receiver of an insolvent insurer to collect on reinsurance contracts. Despite these changes, however, the basic thrust of the regulation of reinsurance is directed at maintaining the financial viability of the ceding insurer. Most of these new regulations do not apply as long as the ceding insurer purchases reinsurance from a company that is licensed in the ceding insurer's state of domicile and therefore regulated by that state.

To enhance the collectibility of reinsurance, several states, including New York, California and Illinois, have issued regulations setting forth minimum standards for letters of credit issued to secure non-admitted reinsurance. New York has issued a similar regulation setting minimum standards for trust funds used to secure non-admitted reinsurance.

The difficulty of collecting reinsurance may be exacerbated when the reinsurance intermediaries responsible for placing the business are in financial trouble. To address this issue, examiners are not allowed to grant credit for reinsurance unless the reinsuring agreement places the risk of intermediary insolvency on the reinsurer (rather than the ceding company). This is now standard practice in the United States. Problems arising from the conduct of reinsurance intermediaries have been set out in detail by the New York Insurance Department in Regulation 98, which requires the licensing of intermediaries and sets substantive standards for the conduct of their affairs. The New York Insurance Department also has promulgated substantive standards for certain types of reinsurance transactions, including loss portfolio transfers.

The accounting profession also is paying increasing attention to standards for analyzing reinsurance transactions. Several years ago the American Institute of Certified Public Accountants issued an audit guide for reinsurance which lays out how an audit of reinsurance transactions should be conducted for both ceding and assuming companies, and sets standards for documentation and recordkeeping with respect to reinsurance transactions. More recently, the accounting profession has become concerned with identifying transactions which appear as reinsurance in form, but which are, in substance, deposit or investment arrangements. They are seeking to identify such transactions and provide an appropriate way of presenting them on financial statements.

The actuarial profession also has begun to make greater demands on reinsurers. Actuaries, whose role in the insurance industry has grown enormously in recent years, have the challenging task of establishing proper reserving and pricing for long-tail business.

Not so long ago, few people outside the insurance industry knew what reinsurance was, and, if they thought about it at all, they assumed that all aspects of the reinsurance business were closely regulated by each state's insurance commissioner or that the business was sufficiently competitive so that general oversight of the way business is conducted was all that was needed. However, the attorneys general of 20 states have brought suit against insurers and reinsurers charging that in important areas of the insurance business there was neither effective regulation nor competition. They believe that, as a result of their legal proceedings, competition will return to the marketplace. Enhanced competition is also the goal of federal legislators who seek to repeal the McCarran-Ferguson Act, which exempts insurers from certain federal antitrust laws. Some think legislators see this move as a relatively quick and easy solution to the problems of insurance availability and affordability which they have been asked to resolve. The repeal of the McCarran-Ferguson Act would obviously be both quick and simple but its effect would be the opposite of what was intended. The sharing of information, which without McCarran-Ferguson Act exemption would violate antitrust laws, enables many small- or medium-sized insurers to write types of business for which they would otherwise have insufficient statistical experience to price on their own. Thus, repeal efforts should be coupled with affirmative legislation which would continue to authorize certain information-sharing and risk-pooling activities. But the uncertainty and conflicts in legal interpretation arising from this new legislation would probably take many years to resolve. Two other approaches to the issues of affordability and availability are removing the current legislative barrier which prevents the Federal Trade Commission from becoming involved in the regulation of insurance, and establishing a federal system of insurance regulation, either as a replacement for state regulation or in tandem with it, much like the current regulatory structure of the banking industry. Thus far, the federal government has been reluctant to become heavily involved in the regulation of the insurance business.

## CHANGES IN MANAGEMENT PHILOSOPHY

The governmental actions described above have taken place largely as a response to the rising demands of insurance buyers. Buyers of primary insurance want availability, simplicity, responsiveness on claims and above all, low cost. Ceding insurers want the same things from their reinsurers. But in seeking to provide this for their clients, the management of a reinsurer must guard against "giving away" its capital. To avoid this pitfall and to cope with the cyclical nature of the reinsurance business, there have been basic changes in management philosophy, including a return to basics. Reinsurers also have been exploring new ways of doing business and some entirely new business ventures. They have established reinsurance intermediaries to better compete with brokers who handle a large share of the total reinsurance premium volume. Reinsurers that formerly concentrated their marketing efforts on direct writing have expanded their role in the brokerage market, even creating separate subsidiaries for this purpose. They also are studying how computers can be used to assist in the underwriting process and to communicate information between ceding and assuming insurers, with a view to enhancing efficiency and flexibility over time.

In line with these broad strategies, reinsurers have been seeking to strengthen their technical expertise. While in the past reinsurance companies had limited staff—people who dealt with clients and a clerical staff to do the bookkeeping—major reinsurers today employ a highly specialized group of professionals, particularly in the areas of underwriting, actuarial science and law. In addition, marketing personnel often have a strong background in the technical aspects of the business. Thus people now moving into key leadership and supervisory roles are likely to be individuals who have moved up the ladder from highly technical areas and who therefore bring considerable technical expertise to these more generalized positions. Other sectors of the financial industry have gone through the same kind of change.

One aspect of the change in ceding company/reinsurer relationships has to do with educating ceding companies about their responsibilities for handling underwriting and claims functions. Most disputed reinsurance claims are resolved by arbitration and therefore leave no published decisions. However, there is a small but growing body of court decisions, resulting from reinsurance disputes, which emphasize the duties of the ceding insurer. These include the proper underwriting of ceded business, properly advising the reinsurer of developments concerning insured business and proper handling of claims. As mentioned in the chapter on loss development, claims handling includes giving the reinsurer prompt notice of claims so that it can exercise its rights with respect to the handling of these claims and fulfill its obligations to properly reserve for them.

Delay in notifying the reinsurers of claims is a major element in the rising number of reinsurance claims disputes. A primary insurer has a broad duty to investigate claims and, under a liability policy, a duty to defend its insured even when the claims are questionable as to merit or coverage. Normally a reinsurer has no such duties to its ceding insurer. It therefore becomes the obligation of the ceding insurer to make a timely and complete presentation of claims to its reinsurer and the failure to do so may be basis for a reinsurer's denial of claims.

These changes in management philosophy indicate an end of the period of "innocence" in reinsurance. In the 1970s and early 1980s, it was commonplace to speak of innocent reinsurance capacity. Reinsurers took whatever was offered in the innocent belief that ceding insurers had properly underwritten the business and that they were bringing reinsurers in as equal partners in underwriting for joint profit (or loss). But what appeared initially to be an honest joint venture sometimes turned out differently. As a result, some reinsurers were financially ruined and those lucky enough to survive were poorer but less naive. Similarly, some innocent ceding companies believed that they would somehow be able to collect on their claims regardless of what they did or told their reinsurers. They took on business that they would never have underwritten had they not thought that they could pass on the underwriting risk to others. Such attitudes have led to concerns about the solvency of primary insurers and the collectibility of their reinsurance.

From the age of innocence, the survivors have emerged, both stronger and wiser. And despite reinsurers' disproportionate share of society's tragic problems, such as asbestos claims, the system has not only survived, but functions well. Reinsurance still performs the basic functions described in the first part of this monograph and there is every reason to expect that it will continue to do so in the future.

# CHAPTER 6

# Alien Reinsurance

By Charles W. Havens III
Partner and
William C. Marcoux
Associate, LeBoeuf, Lamb, Leiby & MacRae, Attorneys

ALIEN REINSURANCE CONSTITUTES an important segment of the reinsurance market for United States insurers.

This chapter will describe the nature and size of the alien reinsurance market, how it operates in the United States, and the changing regulatory and business environment in which these insurers operate.

## WHAT IS THE ALIEN REINSURANCE MARKET?

Alien reinsurers are reinsurers that conduct business in this country but are domiciled in a country other than the United States. They include the largest and some of the most sophisticated reinsurers (six of the 10 largest reinsurers in the world are not domiciled here) as well as some of the smallest and least sophisticated companies. Some are domiciled in countries whose financial standards and regulatory controls for insurers are greater and more restrictive than the United States; others come from countries that impose fewer requirements and regulations on their domestic companies than the United States. In sum, the alien reinsurance market is vast and disparate, and any discussion of its attributes or regulatory reaction to its operations must acknowledge these differences.

Reinsurance has always been an international market. London and Western Europe, particularly Germany and Switzerland, have traditionally been strong reinsurance centers. In the past 10 years, reinsurers from other countries, notably Japan and Scandinavia, have increasingly emerged as prominent players in the reinsurance market.

Because the United States is the largest single reinsurance market in the world, with 1987 premiums of approximately $22.5 billion, alien reinsurers, by necessity and desire, have pursued U.S. business. Today, approximately one-third of the U.S. reinsurance premiums are ceded to alien reinsurers. Furthermore, as the operations of foreign manufacturers in the United States grow, their insurance and reinsurance requirements will increase, thereby providing additional demand and opportunity for alien reinsurers.

Munich Re, the largest reinsurer in the world, epitomizes the sophistication and international nature of the reinsurance industry. Founded in 1880, it now has reinsurance offices in more than 40 cities worldwide and accepts business from insurers in more than 140 countries. In 1987, it had premium income of approximately $6.3 billion (approximately three times the premium income of General Reinsurance Corporation, the largest U.S. reinsurer). Among the other top reinsurers that are also alien insurers are Swiss Re (based in Switzerland and the second largest reinsurer in the world), Mercantile and General Re (based in London), and Underwriters at Lloyd's, London.

## U.S. OPERATIONS OF ALIEN REINSURERS

Alien reinsurers may underwrite business in the United States on a licensed or unlicensed basis. Because of differences in regulatory requirements, accounting practices and tax considerations, most alien reinsurers do not become licensed in this country. Some, however, among them Munich Re and Swiss Re, have established licensed U.S. branches or subsidiaries. As a result, these reinsurers may write business on a licensed and unlicensed basis. Licensed U.S.

branches or subsidiaries of alien reinsurers operate on the same basis as U.S. domiciled companies and are subject to the same panoply of reporting requirements and examinations. Accordingly, the discussion below will address only the operations of unlicensed alien reinsurers which write U.S. business from their domiciliary jurisdiction.

Because of the relative sophistication and bargaining strength of the parties, reinsurance transactions, whether with a domestic, foreign or alien reinsurer, have been relatively free from the regulatory requirements imposed on licensed primary insurers. A U.S. insurer may therefore cede business, directly or through intermediaries or brokers, to an alien reinsurer. U.S. regulators, however, affect substantial control over these transactions by governing when a ceding company may recognize such reinsurance as an asset or reduction from its liabilities on its annual statutory statement (i.e., "take credit" for the reinsurance).

In 1984, the National Association of Insurance Commissioners (NAIC) adopted a model law on credit for reinsurance. Since that time, eight states have adopted this law and approximately 17 others have enacted laws or amended existing laws to make them similar in substantive respects to the model law. Virtually all states have some form of legislation or regulation which governs credit for reinsurance.

The NAIC model credit law, like most credit-for-reinsurance statutes, is primarily concerned with the reinsurers' ability to pay. With regard to unlicensed alien reinsurers, it provides, in pertinent part, that a ceding company cannot take automatic credit for reinsurance ceded to an unlicensed alien reinsurer, unless that reinsurer reports annually to the relevant commissioner information substantially in the form required for the NAIC Annual Statement. In addition, it must also maintain a U.S. trust fund for the payment of valid claims in an amount equal to its U.S. liabilities plus an additional $20 million. In the case of a group of individual unincorporated underwriters, the U.S. trust fund must be in the amount equal to the group's U.S. liabilities plus $100 million. The trust fund must be in a "qualified financial institution" (essentially any state or federally chartered financial institution or licensed U.S. branch or agency office of a foreign banking organization).

If the alien reinsurer does not establish a trust to qualify for credit, and most do not or choose not to, the ceding insurer can take credit for the reinsurance only to the extent that it withholds funds or the reinsurer posts funds to secure its obligations. These funds are most often posted by means of a trust agreement or a clean, irrevocable, unconditional and evergreen (i.e., automatically renewed) letter of credit. The exact form of these trust agreements and letters of credit is governed by various state insurance department requirements, e.g., New York Regulation 133 (for letters of credit) and New York Regulation 114 (for trust agreements).

Because it is essential for most ceding companies to be able to take credit for the reinsurance they cede, credit for reinsurance laws are an effective method of regulating the quality of the reinsurance purchased by U.S. companies. With the exception of requiring certain clauses, the intent of which is to ensure performance under the contract (e.g., a service of suit or insolvency clause), most credit for reinsurance laws do not govern the terms and conditions of the reinsurance transaction. These are properly left to the contracting parties to negotiate.

In addition to credit for reinsurance requirements, in many states various other aspects of the reinsurance transaction are regulated, including the actions of the reinsurance intermediary. Some states also prohibit certain reinsurance arrangements—loss portfolio transfers, for example—and mandate disclosure of certain information regarding reinsurance transactions between affiliate companies.

Finally, reinsurance cessions abroad are subject to a one percent federal excise tax, unless the reinsurer is domiciled in a country which has a reciprocal tax treaty with the United States. At this time, the countries with such treaties include the United Kingdom, France, Italy and Barbados.

## THE CHANGING REGULATORY AND BUSINESS CLIMATE

Over the past several years, regulators have become increasingly concerned about what they view as insufficient control over and information concerning the reinsurance industry in general. The alien reinsurance market has been the subject of special scrutiny, in part because of its importance to U.S. insurers and its geographic distance. As a result, there have been several legislative and regulatory initiatives which affect the operations of alien reinsurers. These include:

1. Establishment by the NAIC's Securities Valuation Office of a list of banks which may issue reinsurance letters of credit. This development, which was intended to subject issuing banks to closer reviews, has had the beneficial impact of expanding the number of banks through which letters of credit may be arranged, thereby enhancing the capacity and price competition for letters of credit.

2. Proposed amendments to NAIC model law on credit for reinsurance, which will increase regulatory requirements, including certain reporting requirements for alien reinsurers which wish to become accredited reinsurers. The proposed amendments to the model law would add, for the first time, a definition of an "accredited reinsurer."

3. Challenges to the current tax treatment of premiums for reinsurance ceded to alien reinsurers.

In attempting to impose additional regulatory requirements on alien reinsurers, legislators and regulators face several legal and practical problems. These include limitations on their extraterritorial reach in monitoring or controlling companies under the supervision of foreign governments, the threat of reciprocal action being taken against U.S. reinsurers trading abroad, and the fact that most alien reinsurers do not, and are not required, to maintain records and accounts in the same format as U.S. insurers.

In an effort to accommodate the competing regulatory requirements, the NAIC has established an International Insurance Relations Task Force to bring together regulators from various countries. The Task Force is currently considering various steps to expand coordination among regulatory bodies, including improving communications and developing a framework for sharing regulatory information. In addition, since the format for reporting financial data in some countries is different from the format used in the United States, the

Task Force is considering ways to facilitate the interpretation of such data.

Concurrent with these regulatory changes, alien reinsurers (and insurers) have become increasingly wary of the unpredictability of their exposure on U.S. business, particularly U.S. general liability business. This unpredictability, which has been evidenced, in part, by judicial decisions and verdicts concerning expansive coverage, joint and several liability, noneconomic damages and punitive damages, has been hotly debated over the past several years and will not be reviewed in detail here. It is proper to say, however, that alien reinsurers remain concerned about U.S. liability business, and their willingness to continue to support the direct underwriting of this business by U.S. insurers will certainly be affected by legislative initiatives and judicial decisions over the next several years. Moreover, as the premium volume for non-U.S. risks increases and as the European Economic Community approaches 1992, the date when many trade barriers to financial services in the European Economic Community are scheduled to disappear, alien reinsurers will have other markets to pursue.

## CONCLUSION

The alien reinsurance market enhances the stability and competitiveness of the U.S. insurance market. It is a dynamic and diversified market. Many of its prominent members have long supported the underwriting activities of U.S. insurers and reinsurers. As the regulatory and business environment changes, it is essential to maintain a proper perspective on the role of the alien reinsurance market.

# CHAPTER 7

Moving Center Stage:

# Reinsurance and Regulation

By James L. Nelson
Former Member, Texas State Board of Insurance, and
Former Chairman, Reinsurance and Anti-Fraud Task Force,
National Association of Insurance Commissioners

THE REINSURANCE BUSINESS, by its very nature, always has been a behind-the-scenes activity. As a form of insurance purchased by insurers rather than the general public, reinsurance is completely unfamiliar to most consumers.

The behind-the-scenes nature of reinsurance is reflected in the fact that, in comparison with primary or direct insurance, reinsurance has received only a limited degree of regulatory attention. Although insurance regulators are well-versed in the business of reinsurance, the focus of insurance regulation has long been upon primary insurers. The idea was that if primary insurers and primary insurance transactions were adequately regulated, the insurance-buying public would be adequately protected.

In addition to licensing and careful financial regulation for solvency, primary insurance regulation usually includes significant oversight of rates, policy forms, and the market conduct of insurers. The activities of insurance agents are regulated through licensing laws. By contrast, reinsurers are usually subjected only to licensing and financial regulation for solvency, and this occurs only if the reinsurer is domiciled in this country. Because much of this country's reinsurance capacity is provided by companies domiciled in other countries, many reinsurers are, in fact, unregulated in this country by the states in which they do business. At the same time, reinsurance intermediaries, who facilitate transactions between insurers and reinsurers, also are generally unregulated.

The absence of direct regulation does not mean that reinsurance has been ignored. Regulators have exercised significant control over reinsurance by controlling the extent to which reinsurance purchased by primary insurers is recognized in the financial statements of the primary insurers. Normally, credit for reinsurance will be recognized by a state only if the reinsurer is licensed in that state or in another state having equal or greater capital and surplus requirements or if the reinsurer's obligations to the primary insurer are backed by deposits, trust funds, or letters of credit. Although this indirect control over the quality of reinsurance does not compare to the level of regulation imposed on primary insurers and insurance transactions, it long has been considered the most appropriate means of protecting the public interest in the area of reinsurance.

However, changes in the insurance and reinsurance marketplace during the last several years have led to changes in the regulatory perception of reinsurance and a greater awareness of the reinsurance business on the part of the public. In many ways, reinsurance has moved from behind the scenes to center stage.

In the early 1980s, indications of fraudulent activity in the reinsurance marketplace and concerns about the collectibility of reinsurance caused regulators to focus greater attention on reinsurance. In 1982, the National Association of Insurance Commissioners formed the Reinsurance and Anti-Fraud Task Force. Regulatory actions in individual states also began to reflect this heightened concern about reinsurance.

Interest in reinsurance grew dramatically in the mid-1980s as this country experienced a liability insurance availability and affordability crisis of unparalleled proportions. The unwillingness of reinsurers to renew some liability reinsurance treaties, or the willingness to do so only at dramatically increased rates, was widely recognized as a major catalyst in the market upheaval. Calls for broader regulation of the reinsurance marketplace began to be heard both within regulatory circles and outside them.

Although the liability insurance crisis is now history, the serious concerns about reinsurance which grew out of the crisis continue to loom large. The potential impact of unrecoverable reinsurance on the solvency of primary insurers is easily the greatest problem. But the possibility that at some time in the future a lack of reinsurance may precipitate a repetition of the crisis or add to its dimensions also weighs heavily in regulators' minds.

The areas in which the NAIC is expanding reinsurance regulation or considering expansion may give the best indication of how regulators view reinsurance today. Changes have already been made in the annual statements filed by insurers and reinsurers domiciled in the United States so that regulators will be able to gather more detailed information about reinsurance as a line of business. Additional changes have been made which increase the amount of security required before credit will be given for reinsurance obtained from unauthorized insurers. Disclosure of reinsurance write-offs and commutations is now required. (Commutation is a process involving the estimation, payment and complete discharge of all current and future obligations between the parties to a reinsurance contract. It may also involve the discounting of future loss payments which will reduce the amount of indebtedness.) Beginning with the 1989 annual statement, "aging" of reinsurance recoverables (information on the degree to which payments are overdue) is required and no credit will be given for some long-outstanding recoverables.

Contemplated expansion of reinsurance regulation is not limited to changes in required financial statements. The NAIC has given some consideration to such possibilities as separate licensing for reinsurers (a primary insurer's license would no longer automatically qualify the insurer to write reinsurance), increasing capital and surplus requirements for reinsurers, and the licensing of reinsurance intermediaries. Efforts are currently underway to strengthen two model laws, the Model Law on Credit for Reinsurance Act and the Model Immunity Act which provides immunity from lawsuits for those reporting information on insurance fraud and those who receive such information.

Direct regulatory involvement in some aspects of individual reinsurance agreements also is being considered in some jurisdictions.

Exactly how reinsurance will be regulated in the years ahead has not been determined yet, but significantly enhanced regulation is assured. Regulators now have a better knowledge and understanding of reinsurance and will be building on this expertise as time goes on. This is certain to increase the effectiveness of reinsurance regulation, whether that regulation continues to focus upon primary insurers and the allowance of credit for reinsurance or is expanded to include more direct oversight of the reinsurance marketplace. Regardless of the shape it takes, reinsurance regulation in the future will clearly reflect the fact that, as a regulatory concern, reinsurance has moved to center stage.

# CHAPTER 8

Recent Annual Statement Changes:

# Improved Reinsurance Data

By James M. Shamberger
Senior Vice President, Reinsurance Association of America

A S THE COMBINED RATIO for reinsurers reported by the Reinsurance Association of America rose more than 20 percentage points in a four-year period, reaching 128.2 in 1984, insurance regulators became increasingly aware of how critical reinsurance was to the solvency of their domestic ceding insurers. And when several reinsurers withdrew from the market, an event that was widely publicized, the question of whether a company's reinsurers would be there, or would respond, when needed, became an issue of major importance. But as their concerns grew, regulators also began to realize that the statutory annual statement did not provide sufficient information on reinsurance to enable them to evaluate the financial condition of the ceding or assuming companies or the extent to which reinsurers were, or were not, meeting their contractual obligations.

The changes that have been made in the annual statement since that time will significantly alter the quantity and quality of reinsurance data available for regulatory use. The purpose of this chapter is to describe some of these changes and the effect they will have on reinsurers and their ceding companies.

## INTRODUCTION

For state insurance regulators, the annual statements adopted by the National Association of Insurance Commissioners (NAIC) constitute the basic tools by which the solvency of insurance companies is verified on an annual basis through insurance department desk audits. These forms adhere to "statutory accounting procedures," an accounting philosophy which is more conservative than the "generally accepted accounting procedures" typically used in public accounting. Property/casualty companies are required to complete the "fire and casualty" annual statement, one of several annual statement forms, usually referred to as blanks, that have been developed to evaluate the financial condition of companies writing various types of insurance or the organizations providing such coverage. (Other blanks cover life, accident and health insurance, title insurance and health maintenance organizations.) Each blank is reviewed annually by the NAIC Blanks Task Force (usually referred to as the Blanks Committee), which is responsible for considering all the numerous proposals for improving the annual statement submitted to it by interested individuals and organizations.

In the 1970s and early 1980s relatively few proposals were submitted to the Blanks Committee concerning reinsurance. However, as the insurance industry moved into the downside of the cycle in the mid-1980s, and the importance of having reinsurance which would respond to its contractual obligations was more widely recognized, serious shortcomings in the way reinsurance data were reported in the annual statement became apparent.

These deficiencies related both to information that would permit analysis of a reinsurer's operations and to data that would signal potential problems in recovering monies due on reinsurance contracts. Several major changes in the way reinsurance data are shown have been adopted in the last few years.

## REPORTING OF PREMIUM AND LOSS DATA

Essential elements in the property/casualty annual statement are the premium and loss data reported on Parts 2, 2A, 2B, 3 and 3A of the Underwriting and Investment Exhibit.

Premium and loss data on the Underwriting Exhibit are provided by line of business, i.e., fire, allied lines, farmowners multiple peril, and so on. Schedules O and P show, by line-of-business, or by groups of such lines, how an insurer's losses have developed—whether an insurer's evaluation of losses in a report year was accurate or whether adverse loss development (see Chapter Four on Loss Development) in subsequent years proved estimates to have been too optimistic. These schedules are used by regulators to determine whether, based on past experience, an insurer has made adequate provision for losses not yet paid. However, for reasons which will be explained later, regulators could not always get a clear picture of loss development from looking at the data on Schedules O and P.

Lines of business are commonly considered to be either short- or long- "tail" lines. Lines of business reported on Schedule O, with the exception of reinsurance and international, were generally short-tail—those on which losses are known and paid relatively quickly, such as fire or earthquake. Prior to 1986, Schedule O called for a two-year loss development period. Long-tail lines, such as workers' compensation and medical malpractice, where losses may not be reported for several years and in some cases, the final payments may not be made for a decade or more, are reported on Schedule P. Part 3 of Schedule P currently tracks incurred losses and paid losses for these lines for seven years. (In the 1989 annual statement a subsequent change will require a 10-year history.)

For primary insurance and first-dollar proportional reinsurance, line-of-business reporting of premium and loss data is the logical format. First-dollar proportional reinsurance is reinsurance in which the reinsurer shares premiums and losses with the ceding company from the first dollar, i.e., the reinsurer's liability is not excess of a retention by the ceding company. Line-of-business reporting is appropriate since first-dollar proportional business, being a percentage of the ceding company's premiums and losses, will have the same loss development characteristics as the primary business reinsured. But line-of-business reporting is not a suitable format for excess-of-loss (non-proportional) reinsurance data. Because of the nature of excess-of-loss reinsurance, the premiums and the loss development patterns associated with those premiums are markedly different from proportional reinsurance. The use of line-of-business reporting for excess-of-loss reinsurance therefore causes distortions in the data that make proper analysis difficult. Two additional problems further complicate the situation. First, there has been no uniformity among the reporting procedures adopted by companies writing reinsurance. Second, almost all of the various reporting procedures have resulted in distortions whenever excess-of-loss reinsurance was written by a primary insurer, or when it was written by a reinsurer that was also writing proportional coverages.

For example, among professional reinsurers, insurers whose business is either principally or exclusively reinsurance, there were two major methods of reporting. Some companies provided premium information on a line-of-business basis. But where multiple-line treaties were involved, because they did not underwrite the risks on a by-line basis, and therefore could not obtain information on the underlying premiums from the ceding companies, some reinsurers were forced to estimate the premium breakdown by line. However, they were able to provide the loss development information, as required on Schedules O and P, because by-line loss data usually were available. These loss development triangles, however, contained a mix of proportional and excess-of-loss reinsurance. As previously noted, this mix of business distorted the development triangles with the result that they were not comparable with the loss development patterns of primary insurers or of reinsurers writing exclusively excess-of-loss reinsurance.

Other professional reinsurers used the "reinsurance" line when they completed the Underwriting Exhibit. Companies using that line provided loss development information on Schedule O (with a two-year loss development period) which was totally inadequate for analysis of reinsurance. Here again, the information provided was a mix of proportional and excess-of-loss reinsurance.

Most primary insurers with reinsurance departments however, reported their reinsurance premiums on a line-of-business basis. But again there were distortions because the resulting loss development information often was derived from a mixture of primary insurance business, and pro rata and excess-of-loss reinsurance business.

Pooling arrangements added another layer of complexity to the problem of analyzing the data. For example, in some cases where a group of affiliated insurance companies had assumed external reinsurance and also had utilized a pooling arrangement to reinsure its own business, premiums written by subsidiary companies were 100 percent reinsured by one company and then proportionally reinsured again through other companies. In such a case, if the intercompany business were reported as reinsurance, as it often was, it would be impossible to derive a true picture of the company's financial condition from the data on the annual statement.

The first regulatory action designed to resolve these problems addressed the lack of loss development provided in Schedule O for those companies filing on the "reinsurance" line. The loss development schedule that was adopted—Schedule O-Part-4—was patterned after a Securities and Exchange Commission disclosure form which required 10-year loss developments on loss and loss expense statistics. This schedule first appeared in the 1986 blank. However this new loss development schedule solved only one of the problems discussed above: the inadequate loss development period. The resulting data still were a mix of a company's proportional and excess-of-loss reinsurance business.

The next step was to develop a system that would allow the data associated with the different types of reinsurance business to be reported separately. This move was taken to eliminate the above-noted distortions that resulted when the proportional and excess-of-loss reinsurance data of professional reinsurers were mixed and when the primary insurance data of primary insurers with reinsurance departments were combined with their reinsurance data. The most often cited problem was the latter situation where an insurer principally involved in writing primary coverages started writing casualty excess-of-loss reinsurance without informing its domiciliary regulator. Since losses are slow to develop in the early years, under-reserving in such cases would not be detected by the regulator. When it did become obvious that something was wrong, the company might not have sufficient surplus both to bolster its reserves and to continue to write new business.

Proportional and excess-of-loss business will be separately

reported in the future. Excess-of-loss premiums and losses on the Underwriting Exhibit will be shown in three new subparts to the reinsurance line (line 30). These subparts will report reinsurance of short-tail, long-tail, and financial (financial guaranty, fidelity, surety, and credit) lines and will be designated lines 30A, 30B, and 30C, respectively. Line 30D will be used for the development of reinsurance business previously reported on line 30 prior to 1988. New loss development schedules similar to Schedule O-Part 4 will be added to Schedule O for reporting 10 years of development data from the new lines, 30A, 30B, and 30C on a prospective basis.

First-dollar proportional reinsurance is reported with primary business by line on the Underwriting Exhibit. Loss development will be shown with direct (primary) business on Schedules O and P. This treatment is appropriate since first-dollar proportional business, being a percentage of the ceding company's premiums and losses, will have the same loss development characteristics as the primary business that has been reinsured. These changes were approved to become effective for the 1988 blank.

Another change, implemented in the 1988 annual statement, required that on Part 2B of the Underwriting Exhibit reinsurance assumed and ceded between affiliates and non-affiliates be separated. This will assist examiners in the evaluation of risk.

A proposal adopted by the NAIC in 1988 will combine Schedules O and P in a new Schedule P for 1989 and subsequent years. While this will result in new designations, the substance of the reinsurance reporting changes described above will remain the same.

## CEDED REINSURANCE INFORMATION

1. *Increased Security Required from Unauthorized Companies:* Schedule F of the annual statement provides detailed information on an insurer's assumed and ceded reinsurance transactions. Schedule F-Part 2 reports security held on account of reinsurance in unauthorized insurers. If an insurer is not authorized and its obligations, such as unearned premiums and paid and unpaid losses recoverable, are not secured, either by funds withheld, trust

funds, letters of credit or some other mechanism, the ceding insurer is required to establish a balance sheet liability (in effect a surplus penalty) for any amounts unsecured.

An unauthorized assuming insurer is an insurer which is neither licensed nor otherwise qualified in a particular jurisdiction. Because of differences in state statutes concerning credit for reinsurance, it is impossible to provide a uniform definition of an unauthorized insurer. While an insurer licensed in a state is always authorized there, some states provide that an insurer licensed in another state meeting certain criteria will also be considered authorized. The term "unauthorized insurer" most often describes an alien insurer, which is not operating in the United States through an established branch.

At the 1984 meeting of the Blanks Committee, several regulators argued for a change in the existing Schedule F-Part 2, which, at that time, did not specifically require security for incurred-but-not-reported IBNR losses. Regulators cited several cases in which they had found during routine examinations substantial amounts of unsecured IBNR due from financially troubled reinsurers. By the time this deficiency was discovered, there was no leverage available to secure it. Although state laws generally required security for all amounts due from unauthorized reinsurers, there was no provision in Schedule F-Part 2 at that time to penalize the surplus of an insurer which had not obtained security for IBNR.

The proposal to require the funding of IBNR, as well as allocated paid and unpaid loss adjustment expenses, was adopted over the objections of the industry. While conceding that IBNR was often significant, particularly in long-tail lines, some argued that insurers computed IBNR on a net (or overall) basis and thus the amount was not broken down and allocated to individual companies. Moreover, current reinsurance contracts did not require that IBNR be funded. Although the Blanks Committee recognized the problem of expired contracts and provided for certain limited grandfathering for these contracts, the implementation of this requirement has caused difficulties for some insurers. In particular, companies have found that alien markets generally refuse to fund IBNR. The business decision to fund or to refuse to fund IBNR may be made for any of several reasons, including cost and uncertainty regarding its calculation. Where funds are not provided, the ceding insurer must either find an admitted reinsurer, where security is not required, or bear the surplus penalty.

2. *Identification of "Suspect" Recoverables:* Regulators' concern about whether ceding companies would be able to collect on their reinsurance contracts became widespread with the much-publicized departure of a number of companies from the reinsurance business when the insurance cycle bottomed out in 1984 and 1985. While there were reports that as many as 100 reinsurers had withdrawn from the market for various reasons, the number of companies actually forced into liquidation was fairly small.

Nonetheless, changing markets and increased doubts about the collectibility of reinsurance led to a Blanks Committee proposal that makes it easier to assess the potential bottom-line impact of amounts due on reinsurance contracts. The proposal requires the identification of certain amounts recoverable from both authorized and unauthorized reinsurers that, because of their particular status, might not be collected. The disclosure, adopted as a new column in Schedule F-Part 1A - Section 1 for the 1987 annual statement, provided for the three distinct classes of funds that might not be collected to be identified by the letter "J", "W", or "S".

The "J" designation indicated that the reinsurer was subject to delinquency proceedings such as rehabilitation, conservation, liquidation, or comparable action. The "W" identification indicated a dispute which had led to the initiation of arbitration or legal action. Finally, the "S" designation represented a recoverable amount where all or part of the balance was 90 days or more past due under the terms of the reinsurance agreement.

Industry representatives argued more about the effectiveness of the disclosure requirement than its substance. For example, it was predicted that companies would defer initiating litigation or arbitration to avoid the "W" disclosure and would amend their contract payment terms to avoid the "S" disclosure of amounts past due. Questions were also raised regarding the use that regulators would make of such information. While there was little objection to the use of the identification as a warning of potential trouble, there was concern that some regulators might require the immediate write-off of all amounts due from affected reinsurers.

3. *Recognition of Potential Unrecoverables:* It was recognized that once information on past due recoverables and recoverables from reinsurers in delinquency proceedings was available, regulators could no longer ignore the potential effect of these balances not being collectible. To encourage uniform treatment, a plan to penalize the surplus of an insurer with certain questionable recoverables was developed. The initial proposal called for the creation of a liability, similar to that required for unsecured obligations of unauthorized reinsurers, for *all* recoverables from a company once *any* recoverable was 90 days or more past due. Since admissible balances from unauthorized reinsurers must be secured, the penalty would have been applicable only to authorized reinsurers.

However, subsequently, when the proposal was revised, both the increased disclosure requirements as well as the penalty aspects of the plan were included. More sophisticated information on past due recoverables would be provided by incorporating an aging feature for both authorized and unauthorized insurers in Schedule F-Part 1A-Section 1. The present column for reinsurance recoverable on paid losses would be supplemented by four columns in which recoverable reinsurance would be shown as current and 1-29 days overdue, overdue 30-90 days, overdue 91-180 days and overdue more than 180 days. This information, which would highlight companies that are slow in paying, would be helpful for ceding insurers as well as for regulators.

Additionally, amounts in a dispute between a ceding company and one or more of its reinsurers which involves "material" recoverables must be disclosed. This will be shown on a new Note to Financial Statements. For the purpose of this requirement, a material recoverable is an amount in excess of 5 percent of the ceding company's policyholders' surplus, if due from a single reinsurer, or an amount in excess of 10 percent of surplus if due from more than one reinsurer. The note also requires the ceding company to classify by company the amount in dispute as being on notice, in arbitration, or in litigation.

These disclosure requirements, which originated from the reinsurance accounting study group, were approved in June 1988 for action by the Blanks Committee in October. The NAIC adopted the proposal for the 1989 blank.

Development of the surplus penalty portion of the proposal was not completed at the NAIC's June meeting; however, the study group subsequently submitted a recommendation for consideration by the Blanks Committee in October. This proposal did not have the weight of the disclosure requirements mentioned above, since it had not been considered by its parent, the Accounting Practices and Procedures Task Force. Because of this technicality, it was deferred to the December NAIC meeting. At that time procedural requirements were met and it was adopted.

If an insurer has recoverables from an authorized reinsurer more than 90 days past due, it must determine, by completing a new Schedule F-Part 2B-Section 1, whether a surplus penalty is to be imposed and, if so, how large. Reinsurance recoverable from a reinsurer that has not paid under the terms of its contract would be shown in two different ways, depending on the ratio of amounts past due to the total amount recoverable from that reinsurer together with the amounts received from it within the past 90 days. If the ratio of amounts over 90 days past due (excluding amounts in dispute) divided by the total reinsurance recoverable from that reinsurer on paid losses (excluding amounts in dispute) and amounts received in the past 90 days, is less than 20 percent, the amount over 90 days past due (excluding amounts in dispute) would be shown in a column for reinsurers showing a ratio of less than 20 percent past due reinsurance recoverable. If the ratio is 20 percent or greater, the potential effect and implications would be more serious. In such a case, all recoverables due from that reinsurer (including unearned premiums, paid and unpaid losses, paid and unpaid allocated loss adjustment expenses and IBNR) would be shown on a new Schedule F-Part 2B-Section 2. A formula for calculating the penalty to be imposed for overdue authorized reinsurance calls for the addition of amounts due from both sources: all reinsurance companies in the ratio-of-less-than-20-percent past due column together with amounts due from all those with a ratio of 20 percent or higher past due. A reduction would be permitted for funds held or any other type of security against balances reported on Schedule F-Part 2B-Section 2. To begin with, for the 1989 blank, the surplus penalty would be equal to 20 percent of that total.

The 1989 penalty of 20 percent represents a phasing-in of the requirements. The study group has not made any projections as to the ultimate amount because at this time it is difficult to assess the potential impact of the surplus penalty.

4. *Write-Off of Uncollectible Reinsurance:* While there is recognition of the need to identify reinsurance which may not be collectible, no standards currently exist for determining when and how a recoverable must be written off. While a prudent insurer would presumably write off collectibles as their recovery became increasingly unlikely, such an assumption is less valid if the ceding insurer itself is in precarious financial condition.

The potential for widely differing treatment, and inappropriate treatment in instances where early action should be taken, support regulatory action to define when recoverables should be written off. This appears to be the next logical step now that potential unrecoverable reinsurance is being identified and subjected to a surplus penalty.

These recent changes in the annual statement will have a considerable impact on the effectiveness of reinsurance regulation. First, they will make it easier to evaluate two key factors that have a significant bearing on an insurer's financial condition: the adequacy of a company's reserves for losses not yet paid and the extent to which its reinsurers are meeting their contractual obligations.

Second, they will force some ceding companies to readjust their criteria for purchasing reinsurance. Because overdue reinsurance will now be identified and a penalty applied to the ceding company's surplus where outstanding amounts of reinsurance are significant, insurers will be more likely to deal with reinsurers that are willing and able to pay promptly. This, in turn, will enhance the financial stability of the insurance industry in general.

# Insurance and Reinsurance Terms

The definitions listed below are taken primarily from the glossary included in the textbook, "Reinsurance," edited by Robert W. Strain, CLU, CPCU, and published by Strain Publications, Wingdale, NY.

**Acquisition Costs**—The cost to an insurer of securing business, such as advertising, sales promotion and agent's and broker's commissions.

**Admitted Assets**—Assets recognized and accepted by state insurance laws in determining the solvency of insurers or reinsurers.

**Admitted Company**—(1) An insurer licensed to conduct business in a given state. (2) A reinsurer licensed or approved to conduct business in a given state.

**Aggregate Excess-of-Loss Reinsurance**—A form of excess-of-loss reinsurance which indemnifies the ceding company against the amount by which the ceding company's losses incurred during a specific period (usually 12 months) exceed either (1) a predetermined dollar amount or (2) a percentage of the company's base premiums for the specific period. This is commonly referred to as stop-loss reinsurance or excess-of-loss ratio reinsurance.

**Alien Company**—An insurance company organized under the laws of a foreign country.

**Annual Statement**—A summary of an insurance company's (or reinsurer's) financial operations for a particular year, including a balance sheet supported by detailed exhibits and schedules, filed with the state insurance department of each jurisdiction in which the company is licensed to conduct business. Also known as convention blank or convention statement.

**Assume**—To accept all or part of a ceding company's insurance or reinsurance on a risk or exposure.

**Attachment Point**—The amount at which excess reinsurance protection becomes operative; the retention under an excess reinsurance contract.

**Authorized Reinsurance**—Reinsurance placed with a reinsurer which is licensed or otherwise recognized by a particular state insurance department.

**Base Premium**—The ceding company's premiums (written or earned) to which the reinsurance premium rate is applied to produce the reinsurance premium.

**Capacity**—The measure of an insurer's financial strength to issue contracts of insurance, usually determined by the largest amount acceptable on a given risk or, in certain other situations, by the maximum volume of business it is prepared to accept.

**Catastrophe**—In insurance, a term applied for statistical recording purposes to an incident or series of related incidents involving an insured loss expected to exceed $5 million.

**Catastrophe Reinsurance**—A form of excess-of-loss reinsurance which, subject to a specific limit, indemnifies the ceding company against the amount of loss in excess of a specified retention. This loss amount represents the accumulation of losses resulting from a catastrophic event or series of events.

**Cede**—To transfer to a reinsurer all or part of the insurance or reinsurance written by a ceding company with the object of reducing the potential liability of the latter.

**Ceding Commission**—In reinsurance, an allowance (usually a percentage of the reinsurance premium) made by the reinsurer for part or all of a ceding company's acquisition and other costs. The ceding commission may also include a profit factor.

**Ceding Company**—An insurance company which cedes all or part of the insurance or reinsurance it has written to another insurer. A company that has placed reinsurance as distinguished from a company that accepts it. Also known as the reinsured.

**Cession**—The unit of insurance passed to a reinsurer by the primary company which issued a policy to the original insured. A cession accordingly may be the whole or a portion of single risks, defined policies or defined divisions of business, as agreed in the reinsurance contract.

**Combined Ratio**—The arithmetic sum of two ratios: incurred loss to earned premium, and incurred expense to written premium. Considered the best simple index to the current underwriting performance of an insurer. Also known as operating ratio.

**Convention Statement**—Another name for the annual statement form of National Association of Insurance Commissioners (NAIC). Also known as convention blank. The term "convention" is derived from the original name for the NAIC which was the National Convention of Insurance Commissioners.

**Direct Writer**—(1) In reinsurance, a reinsurer which negotiates with a ceding company without benefit of an intermediary or broker. (2) In insurance, a primary insurer that sells insurance through licensed agents who produce business essentially for no one else.

**Domestic Company**—An insurer conducting business in its domiciliary state from which it received its charter to write insurance (as opposed to a foreign company: an insurer conducting business in a state other than its domiciliary state; or an alien company: one domiciled outside the United States but conducting business within the United States).

**Earned Premium**—The portion of a premium which is the property of an insurance company, based on the expired portion of the policy period.

**Excess-of-Loss Ratio Reinsurance**—See Aggregate Excess-of-Loss Reinsurance.

**Excess-of-Loss Reinsurance**—A generic term describing reinsurance which, subject to a specified limit, indemnifies the ceding company against all or a portion of the amount in excess of a specified retention.

**Excess-per-Risk Reinsurance**—A form of excess-of-loss reinsurance which, subject to a specified limit, indemnifies the ceding company against the amount of loss in excess of a specified retention with respect to each risk involved in each loss.

**Exposure**—The state of being subject to the possibility of loss; the extent of risk as measured by various standards such as payroll, gate receipts and area.

**Facultative Reinsurance**—The reinsurance of part or all of (the insurance provided by) a single policy in which each cession is negotiated separately. The primary company and the reinsurer have the option of accepting or declining each individual submission (as distinguished from the obligation to cede and accept to which the parties agree in treaty reinsurance).

**Guaranty Fund**—A fund, supported by assessments against solvent insurance companies, to absorb losses of claimants against insolvent insurers.

**Foreign Company**—An insurer conducting business in a state other than its domiciliary state.

**Incurred But Not Reported (IBNR)**—The liability for future payments on losses which have already occurred but have not yet been reported to the reinsurer. This definition may be extended to include expected future development on claims already reported. See Loss Development.

**Incurred Losses**—(1) In insurance accounting, an amount representing the losses paid plus the change (positive or negative) in outstanding loss reserves within a given period of time. (2) Losses which have happened and which will result in a claim under the terms of an insurance policy or a reinsurance agreement.

**Intermediary**—A reinsurance broker who negotiates contracts of reinsurance on behalf of the reinsured, receiving a commission for placement and other services rendered.

**Lead Reinsurer**—The reinsurer recognized as the one of several reinsurers on a contract responsible for negotiating the initial terms of the contract.

**Line**—(1) Either the limit of insurance to be written which a company has fixed for itself on a class of risk (line limit), or the actual amount which it has accepted on a single risk or other unit. (2) A class or type of insurance (fire, marine or casualty, among others), also known as line of business. (3) The word "line" in reinsurance usually pertains to surplus reinsurance and means the amount of the reinsured's retention as respects each risk.

**Lloyd's**—Groups of individuals, called syndicates (not insurance companies), assuming liability through an underwriter. Each individual independently and personally assumes a proportionate part of the risk accepted by the underwriter. Generally refers to Lloyd's of

London, England, where the Lloyd's Corporation provides the support facility for the group's activities.

**Long-Tail Liability**—A term used to describe certain types of third-party liability exposures (e.g., malpractice, products, errors and omissions) where the incidence of loss and the determination of damages are frequently subject to delays which extend beyond the term the insurance or reinsurance is in force. An example would be the contamination of a food product which occurs when the material is packed but which is not discovered until the product is consumed months or years later.

**Loss Development**—The difference between the estimated amount of loss as initially reported to the reinsurer and the estimated amount at a later date or the amount paid in final settlement.

**Loss Ratio**—Losses incurred expressed as a percentage of earned premiums.

**Loss Reserve**—For an individual loss, an estimate of the amount the insurer expects to pay for the reported claim. For total losses, estimates of expected payments for reported and unreported claims. May include amounts of loss adjustment expenses. See Incurred But Not Reported (IBNR) and Incurred Losses.

**Loss Reserve Transfer**—A type of reinsurance treaty through which companies can exchange certain types of liabilities. Also known as loss portfolio transfer.

**Manager**—In reinsurance, any person, partnership or corporation representing an insurer or reinsurer and underwriting for the insurer's or reinsurer's account.

**Net Retention**—The amount of insurance which an insurer keeps for its own account and does not reinsure in any way.

**Nonadmitted Assets**—Assets owned by an insurance company which are not recognized for solvency purposes by state insurance laws or insurance department regulations, e.g., premiums due and uncollected past 90 days, and furniture and fixtures, among others.

**Nonadmitted Company**—(1) An insurer not licensed in a given state. (2) A reinsurer not licensed or approved in a given state.

**Nonadmitted Reinsurance**—Reinsurance protection bought by a ceding company from a reinsurer not licensed or authorized to transact the particular line of business in the jurisdiction in question. No credit is given the ceding company for such nonadmitted reinsurance in its annual statement unless it withholds funds or holds a letter of credit on behalf of such unauthorized reinsurer.

**Non-Proportional Reinsurance**—Reinsurance under which the reinsurer's participation in a loss depends on the size of the loss. Also known as excess-of-loss reinsurance.

**Occurrence**—(1) An event that results in an insured loss. In some lines of insurance, such as liability, it is distinguished from an accident in that the loss does not have to be sudden and fortuitous. It can result from continous or repeated exposure. (2) In reinsurance, per occurrence coverage permits all losses arising out of one event to be aggregated instead of being handled on a risk-by-risk basis.

**Per Risk Reinsurance**—Reinsurance in which the reinsurance limit and the retention apply "per risk" rather than per accident, per event, or in the aggregate.

**Policyholders' Surplus**—(1) The net worth of an insurer as reported in its annual statement. For a stock insurer, the sum of its surplus and capital. For a mutual insurer, its surplus. (2) The amount by which the assets of an insurer exceed the organization's liabilities. Another name for surplus to policyholders.

**Pool**—Any joint underwriting operation of insurance or reinsurance in which the participants assume a predetermined and fixed interest in all business written. Pools are often independently managed by professionals with expertise in the classes of business undertaken, and the members share equally in the premiums, losses, expenses and profits. An "association" and a "syndicate" (excluding that of Lloyd's of London) are both synonymous with a pool, and the basic principles of operation are much the same.

**Primary**—An adjective applied in reinsurance to these nouns: insurer, insured, policy and insurance—meaning respectively: (1) the primary insurer is the insurance company which initially originates the business, i.e., the ceding company; (2) the primary insured is the policyholder insured by the primary insurer; (3) the primary policy is the initial policy issued by the primary insurer to the primary insured; (4) the primary insurance is the insurance covered under the primary policy issued (sometimes called "underlying insurance").

**Professional Reinsurer**—A term used to designate an organization whose business is mainly reinsurance and related services, as contrasted with other insurance organizations which may operate reinsurance-assuming departments in addition to their basic primary insurance business.

**Pro Rata Reinsurance**—A generic term describing all forms of reinsurance in which the reinsurer shares a proportional part of the original losses and premiums of the ceding company. Also known as participating reinsurance and proportional reinsurance.

**Quota-Share Reinsurance**—A form of pro rata reinsurance (proportional) in which the reinsurer assumes an agreed percentage of each insurance being reinsured and shares all premiums and losses accordingly with the reinsured.

**Rate**—The percentage or factor applied to the ceding company's base premium to produce the reinsurance premium, or the percentage applied to the reinsurer's premium to produce the commission payable to the primary company (or, if applicable, the reinsurance intermediary).

**Reciprocity**—The mutual exchanging of reinsurance, often in equal amounts, from one party to another, the object of which is to stabilize overall results.

**Reinsurance**—The transaction whereby the reinsurer, for a consideration, agrees to indemnify the ceding company against all or part of the loss which the latter may sustain under the policy or policies which it has issued.

**Reinsurance Commission**—Another name for ceding commission.

**Reinsurance Premium**—An amount paid by the ceding company to the reinsurer in consideration for liability assumed by the reinsurer.

**Reinsured**—See Ceding Company.

**Reinsurer**—An organization which assumes the liability of another by way of reinsurance.

**Retention**—The amount which an insurer assumes for its own account. In pro rata contracts, the retention may be a percentage of the policy limit. In excess-of-loss contracts, the retention is a dollar amount of loss.

**Retrocession**—The transaction whereby a reinsurer cedes to another reinsurer all or part of the reinsurance it has previously assumed.

**Risk**—The chance of loss. Also used to refer to the insured or to property covered by a policy. In reinsurance, each company makes its own rules for defining units of hazard or single risks.

**Social Inflation**—The increasing of insurance losses caused by higher jury awards, more liberal treatment of claims by workers' compensation boards, legislated rises in benefit levels (in some cases retroactively), and new concepts of tort and negligence, among others.

**Stop-Loss Reinsurance**—See Aggregate Excess-of-Loss.

**Surplus-Share Reinsurance**—A form of pro rata reinsurance indemnifying the ceding company against loss for the surplus liability ceded. Essentially, this can be viewed as a variable quota share contract wherein the reinsurer's pro rata share of insurance on individual risks will increase as the amount of insurance increases, in order that the primary company can limit its net exposure regardless of the amount of insurance written.

**Surplus to Policyholders**—(1) The net worth of an insurer as reported in its annual statement. For a stock insurer, the sum of its unassigned surplus and capital. (2) The amount by which the assets of an insurer exceed the organization's liabilities. Another name for policyholders' surplus.

**Syndicate**—A group of insurers or underwriters who join to insure property that presents high values or high hazards. Also see Pool.

**Treaty**—A reinsurance agreement between the ceding company and the reinsurer, usually for one year or longer, which stipulates the technical particulars applicable to the reinsurance of some class or classes of business.

**Treaty Reinsurance**—A standing agreement between reinsured and reinsurer for the cession and assumption of certain risks as defined in the treaty.

**Umbrella Liability**—A form of insurance protection against losses in excess of the amount covered by other liability insurance policies; also protects the insured in many situations not covered by the usual liability policies.

**Unauthorized Insurer, Reinsurer**—An insurer not licensed, or a reinsurer neither licensed nor approved, in a designated jurisdiction.

**Unauthorized Reinsurance**—Reinsurance placed with a reinsurer which does not have authorized status in the jurisdiction in question.

**Underwriting Capacity**—The maximum amount of money an insurer or reinsurer is willing to risk in a single loss event on a single risk or in a given period. The limit of capacity for an insurer or reinsurer may also be imposed by law or regulatory authority.

**Unearned Premium Reserve**—The sum of all the premiums representing the unexpired portions of the policies or contracts which the insurer or reinsurer has on its books as of a certain date. It is usually based on a formula of averages of issue dates and the length of term.

**Write**—To insure, to underwrite, or to accept an application for insurance.

# Information on Reinsurance

## Associations

Reinsurance Association of America
1819 L Street, N.W., Seventh Floor
Washington, DC 20036
(202) 293-3335

Insurance Information Institute
110 William Street
New York, NY 10038
(212) 669-9200

## Reading List

Brown, Robert H. and Reed, Peter B. ■ *Marine Reinsurance*. London: Witherby & Co. Ltd., 1981.
Carter, Robert L. ■ *Reinsurance*. 2nd ed. Brentford, England: Kluwer Publishing Co., 1983.
*Extent of Reinsurance Use and Cost of Reinsurance Versus Benefit*. ■ Hartford, Conn.: Conning & Co., 1981.
Gerathewohl, Klaus et al. ■ *Reinsurance Principle and Practice*. Karlsruhe, West Germany: Verlag Vericherungswirtschaft e.v., 1980. 2 vols.
Kiln, Robert. ■ *Reinsurance in Practice*. 2nd ed. London: Witherby & Co. Ltd., 1986.
Neave, Julius A. ■ *Speaking of Reinsurance*. Brentford, England: Kluwer Publishing Co., 1980.
Reinsurance Association of America. ■ *Reinsurance Underwriting Review*. Washington D.C.: Reinsurance Association of America, April 1988.
"Reinsurance Intermediaries." ■ *Business Insurance*. October 31, 1988: 3.
"Reinsurance Review." ■ *National Underwriter*. August 29, 1988: Section II.
Strain, Robert. ■ *Reinsurance*. Wingdale, N.Y.: Strain Publications, 1980.
----. *Reinsurance Directory*. ■ Wingdale, N.Y.: Strain Publications, 1988.
----. *Reinsurance Practices: A Workbook with Cases*. ■ Wingdale, N.Y.: Strain Publications, 1982.

# Index

## IIII A

ACCIDENT AND HEALTH INSURANCE, 88
ACCIDENT-YEAR-OF-BUSINESS LOSS COSTS, 40, 52
ACCOUNT EXECUTIVES, 28, 29
ACCOUNTING PRACTICES
  intermediary's role and, 36
  regulators' concern about, 71
  reinsurance transactions and, 73
  statutory vs. generally accepted, 88
  taxes and, 71
  when premium volume increases, 15–17
ACCOUNTING PRACTICES AND PROCEDURES TASK FORCE, 96
ACCREDITED REINSURER, 81
ACQUISITION EXPENSES, 15, 17
ACTUARIAL DEPARTMENT/ACTUARIES, 28, 73
  function of, 40–41
  primary objective of, 51
  professionals in, 75
  losses and, 37
ACTUARIAL SCIENCE, 75
AGGREGATE REINSURANCE AGREEMENT, 20, 23
AGING OF RECEIVABLES, 72, 85, 95
ALIEN REINSURANCE, 70, 77–82, 93
AMERICAN INSTITUTE OF CERTIFIED PUBLIC ACCOUNTANTS, 73
ANALYSES OF LOSS RESERVES AND CLAIMS, 38
ANNUAL REPORTS/STATEMENTS, 27, 31
  actuarial department and, 41
  claims and, 38
  conceptualization and, 33
  lack of sufficient information in, 87, 88
  new requirements regarding, 72, 85, 87–97
  for property/casualty companies, 88–89
ANTITRUST LAWS, 66, 74
ARBITRATION, 27, 75, 94
ASBESTOS-RELATED CLAIMS, 45, 46, 61, 76
  example of trend in, 55
ATTORNEYS GENERAL, 73
AUDIT, CLAIMS, 39
AUDIT GUIDE, 73
AUTHORIZATION (BY INTERMEDIARY), 34

AUTHORIZED INSURER, 92, 94, 95, 96
AUTOMOBILE LIABILITY CLAIMS, 42, 43
  example of trend in, 45, 47, 52, 53
  factors in changing patterns of, 45

## IIII B

BALANCE SHEET LIABILITY, 93
BALANCED PORTFOLIOS, 26
BALANCING ACCOUNTS/BALANCE SHEET, 17, 18, 40
BANKS, 25, 68, 69–70
BINDING, 29
BLACK LUNG DISEASE, 46
BLANKS, 88
BLANKS COMMITTEE, 88, 93, 94, 96
BLANKS TASK FORCE, 88
BOYCOTT, 66
BROKER, 26, 28, 75
  competition and, 68–69
  intermediary's survey and, 32
  layering and, 34
BROKER-OF-RECORD LETTER, 34
BUICK MOTOR CO., 63

## IIII C

CAPACITY
  conceptualization and, 33
  premium-volume, 13, 32
  underwriting, 12–13
CAPITAL, SOURCES OF, 68
CAPITAL ADEQUACY REQUIREMENTS, 70
CAPITAL STRUCTURE, 59, 67
CAPTIVES, 66
CARTER ADMINISTRATION, 70
CASE INVENTORY, 33
CASE–BASIS RESERVES, 39–40
CASH-FLOW UNDERWRITING, 69
CASUALTY COMPANIES, 68, 88
CASUALTY EXCESS-OF-LOSS REINSURANCE, 41, 42
  leverage effect of inflation in, 57
  RAA study and, 51
CATASTROPHIC LOSSES, 12, 15, 34
  claims reporting of, 38
  conceptualization and protection against, 33
  excess-of-loss agreement and, 23
  *See also* Earthquakes
CEDING COMMISSION, 15, 17

CEDING COMPANIES, 11, 26, 65
   changes in relationships with, 59, 75
   choice between brokerage and non-
     brokerage market by, 28
   claims audit of, 39
   credit for reinsurance, 80
   facultative reinsurance and, 64
   increased size of retention of, 64
   new information requirements for,
     92–97
   recognition of potential
     unrecoverables and, 95
   reserving practices of, 40
   responsibilities of, 75
   rising expectations of reinsurance
     industry by, 71
CENTER RE, 68
CERTIFIED PUBLIC ACCOUNTANTS, 35
CLAIMS
   intermediary's role and, 32, 33, 36
   legal defense of, 38
   payouts, increased, 60
   See also Claims department;
     Reporting claims
CLAIMS AUDIT, 39
CLAIMS DEPARTMENT
   losses and, 37, 37–40
   prompt reporting by, 38, 75–76. See
     also Reporting claims, delay in
CLAIMS-MADE POLICY, 64–65, 72
COERCION, 66
COLLECTIBILITY (OF REINSURANCE),
   71, 72, 76, 84
   new annual statement requirements
     and, 94–97
COMMERCIAL BANKS, 25, 68, 69–70
COMMISSIONS, 15, 17
   under quota-share agreements, 20
COMMUTATIONS, 85
COMPARATIVE NEGLIGENCE, 45, 60
COMPETITION
   in financial markets, 70
   in reinsurance market, 59, 67–69,
     73–74
COMPUTERS, TO AID UNDERWRITING,
   75
CONCEPTUALIZATION (BY
   INTERMEDIARY), 33, 34
CONTACT (BY INTERMEDIARY), 31
CONTRACTS, 11, 64–65
   arbitration panels and, 27
   cancellation of, 19
   excess-of-loss ratio, 23

   intermediary's role and, 35
   reinsurance vs. other types, 27
   separate ones negotiated, 24
   stop-loss, 23
   See also Contractual obligations;
     Facultative reinsurance; Treaty
     reinsurance
CONTRACTUAL OBLIGATIONS, 87, 88,
   97
CONTRIBUTORY NEGLIGENCE, 45, 60
CONVENTION STATEMENTS, 31
   SEE ALSO ANNUAL REPORTS/
   STATEMENTS
COST-EFFECTIVE REINSURANCE, 33,
   34
COURT OF APPEALS OF STATE OF NEW
   YORK, 63
CREDIT FOR REINSURANCE, 79, 81, 84,
   85
   new requirements concerning, 93

## ‖‖‖ D

DATA BASE, INADEQUATE, 14
DATA PROCESSING, 36
DEBRIS CLEANUP PROVISIONS, 61
DEDUCTIBLE, IN EXCESS-OF-LOSS
   REINSURANCE, 19
DIRECT (NON-BROKERAGE)
   REINSURANCE WRITER, 28–30, 68,
   75
DISCOUNTING LOSS RESERVES, 71, 85
DISTRIBUTION SYSTEMS, 28–30
DIVERSIFICATION, 14, 29
   geographic, and catastrophic losses,
     15
   intermediary's role and, 33, 35–36
   reciprocity, 26
DOCUMENTATION (OF REINSURANCE
   TRANSACTIONS), 73

## ‖‖‖ E

EARTHQUAKES, 62
EMERGENCE
   defined, 52
   slow, 42, 52
   of medical malpractice claims, 46
EMERGENCE CURVES, 42, 43–45, 46
   by line of business, 42, 43
   for primary vs. reinsurance, 52–58
EUROPEAN ECONOMIC COMMUNITY, 82
EVERGREEN LETTER OF CREDIT, 80

EXCESS BOND REINSURANCE
ASSOCIATION, 25
EXCESS-OF-LOSS (NON-
PROPORTIONAL) REINSURANCE, 19,
22–23
claims reporting and, 38, 39
conceptualization and, 33
data distortions and, 90, 91
IBNR vs. reported reserves and, 41
layering and, 23–25
mixed with pro rata and primary, 90,
91
reporting of premium and loss data,
89–90, 92
reserving and, 40
shift from pro rata to, 64
*See also* Casualty excess-of-loss
reinsurance
EXCESS-OF-LOSS RATIO CONTRACT, 23
EXPENSES (OF COMPANY), 33

## F

FACULTATIVE REINSURANCE, 19, 24,
26
increased risk exposure and growth
in, 63–64
ratio to treaty, 27
FAIR SETTLEMENT COST, 38
FEDERAL TRADE COMMISSION, 74
FIDELITY & DEPOSIT COMPANY VS.
PINK, 72
FINANCIAL DATA (OF COMPANY), 87–97
distortions in, 90, 91
intermediary's survey and, 33
FINANCIAL MARKETS, 69–70
FINANCIAL STATEMENTS, 84. *SEE ALSO*
ANNUAL REPORTS/STATEMENTS;
BALANCING ACCOUNTS/BALANCE
SHEET
FINANCING (BY REINSURANCE), 12,
15–17, 18
cash flow diagram showing, 15, 16
FINITE RISK REINSURANCE, 65
FIRE AND CASUALTY STATEMENT, 88
FIRST-DOLLAR PROPORTIONAL
REINSURANCE, 89, 92
FOLLOW–UP PROCEDURES (OF
COMPANY), 33
FRAUD, 84, 85
FUTURE PLANS (OF COMPANY), 33

## G

GENERAL LIABILITY CLAIMS, 42, 43
example of trend in, 49, 52, 55
products liability included in, 45
GENERAL REINSURANCE
CORPORATION, 65, 78
GEOGRAPHIC DIVERSIFICATION, 14, 15
GLOBALIZATION OF INDUSTRIES, 60
GOVERNMENT-OWNED REINSURANCE
COMPANIES, 25
GRANDFATHERING OF CONTRACTS, 93
GUEST STATUTES, 45

## H

HAZARDOUS OPERATIONS, 19
HAZARDOUS WASTES, 61
HEALTH MAINTENANCE
ORGANIZATIONS, 88
HUMAN CAPITAL, 68

## I

IBNR (INCURRED BUT NOT REPORTED)
LOSSES. *SEE* INCURRED BUT NOT
REPORTED (IBNR) LOSSES
IDENTIFICATION OF SUSPECT
RECOVERABLES, 94–95
INCURRED BUT NOT REPORTED (IBNR)
LOSSES, 33, 37
claims audit and, 39–40
determining reserves for, 40
as difference between ultimate loss
costs and reported losses thus far,
40–41
not included in emergence, 52
security for, 93
INDEX FACTOR, 51
INDEXING, 51, 70
INDIVIDUAL REINSURANCE
AGREEMENT, 20, 23, 85
INDIVIDUAL RISK, 12–13, 19. *SEE ALSO*
FACULTATIVE REINSURANCE
INFLATIONARY EFFECTS
on automobile and general liability,
45, 57
indexing and, 51
on reinsurance industry, 70
INJURIES, 46, 61
INNOCENT REINSURANCE CAPACITY,
76

INSOLVENCY, 71, 73
  clause, 72, 80
  policyholders' surplus and, 17
  as response to increased risk
    exposure, 65
INSURANCE SERVICES OFFICE, 14, 67
INTEREST RATE VOLATILITY, 69
INTERMEDIARY, 26, 28, 75
  vs. account executive, 29–30
  insolvency of, 72–73
  regulation of conduct/actions of, 73,
    80, 84
  reinsurance market and, 34, 35
  role of, 31–36
  See also Broker
INTERNATIONAL INSURANCE
  RELATIONS TASK FORCE, 81
INTIMIDATION, 66

## ‖‖ J

J FUNDS, 94
JOINT AND SEVERAL LIABILITY, 60
JURY AWARDS, 60

## ‖‖ L

LARGER INSURANCE COMPANIES, 30
LAW OF LARGE NUMBERS, 13
LAWS/LEGISLATION, 27
  proposed new, 74, 85
  state, 27, 93
  See also Regulation(s)
LAYERING/LAYERS, 23–25, 34, 64
  inflation and higher, 70
LEAD QUOTATIONS, 34
LEGAL ENVIRONMENT
  changes in, 60, 62, 80–82, 84
  lack of predictability of, 63
  reduced margin for error in, 66–67
LEGAL TECHNICAL SUPPORT, 38, 75
LETTERS OF CREDIT, 70, 72, 84, 93
  alien reinsurers and, 80, 81
LEVERAGE, 51, 57, 93
LIABILITY, 12, 85
  claims audit and, 39–40
  conceptualization and, 33
  loss and loss expense reserves, 37
  net retained, 14
  pro rata reinsurance and, 22
  products, 45, 60, 64
  ratio of retained to ceded, 20
  rule of joint and several, 60

of small vs. large companies, 12–13
  See also Automobile liability claims;
    General liability claims;
    Negligence
LICENSING, 27, 83, 93
  of alien reinsurers, 78–79, 83–84
  to enter new states, 33
  of intermediaries, 73
  of primary insurers, 83
LIFE INSURANCE, 88
LIMITS (ON POLICIES), 12, 70
LIMITS PROFILE, 32
LINE LOSS COSTS, 40
LINE-OF-BUSINESS REPORTING, 42, 43,
  51, 89
  distortions caused by, 90, 91
LINES (IN SURPLUS-SHARE
  AGREEMENT), 22
LLOYD'S, 25, 78
LONG-TAIL RESERVES, 51, 62, 69, 93
  vs. short-, 89, 92
  taxes and, 71
LOSS CONTROL SPECIALISTS, 28
LOSS DEVELOPMENT, 37–58, 89
  defined, 37
  historic patterns of, 40, 42. See also
    Loss development patterns
  new requirements concerning, 72
LOSS DEVELOPMENT PATTERNS, 37, 40
  in 1990s, 46
  distorted, 90, 91
  factors contributing to changes in,
    45–46
  importance of, 42
  by line of business, 42, 43, 51
  primary and reinsurance compared,
    51–58
  of proportional vs. non–proportional
    reinsurance, 89–90
  tail of, 42, 43, 89
LOSS DEVELOPMENT TRIANGLES, 90
LOSS PORTFOLIO TRANSFERS, 73, 80
LOSS RESERVE ADEQUACY. SEE
  RESERVE ADEQUACY
LOSSES, 37–58
  accumulated, 14
  collection and transmission of, 35
  incurred but not reported (IBNR).
    See Incurred but not reported
    (IBNR) losses
  on individual policies, 13
  in pro rata reinsurance, 21
  reported thus far vs. ultimate, 40–41

## M

MACPHERSON VS. BUICK MOTOR CO., 63

MALPRACTICE CLAIMS. *SEE* MEDICAL MALPRACTICE CLAIMS

MANAGEMENT PHILOSOPHY
about risk, 33, 39
changes in, 59, 74–76
*See also* Philosophies (of company)

MATERIAL RECOVERABLES, 95

MCCARRAN-FERGUSON ACT, 66, 74

MEDICAL EXPENSE INFLATION, 45

MEDICAL MALPRACTICE CLAIMS, 42, 43
example of trend in, 50, 52, 56
factors in changing pattern of, 46
slow emergence of, 46, 89

MERCANTILE AND GENERAL RE, 78

MISSION INSURANCE GROUP, 65

MODEL CREDIT LAW, 79, 81, 85

MODEL IMMUNITY ACT, 85

MODEL LAW ON CREDIT FOR REINSURANCE ACT, 85

MULTIPLE-LINE TREATIES, 90

MUNICH RE, 78

MUNICIPAL LIABILITY, 61–62

MUTUAL ATOMIC ENERGY REINSURANCE POOL, 25

## N

NATIONAL ASSOCIATION OF INSURANCE COMMISSIONERS (NAIC), 31, 43, 71, 79
Accounting Practices and Procedures Task Force, 96
Blanks Task Force, 88, 96
International Insurance Relations Task Force, 81
Reinsurance and Anti–Fraud Task Force, 84
Securities Valuation Office, 81
state insurance regulators and, 88

NEGLIGENCE
change from contributory to comparative, 45, 60
liability vs. strict liability, 60

NET RETAINED LIABILITY, 14

NET RETENTION, 14, 19, 22. *SEE ALSO* RETENTION

NEW AREAS (DIVERSIFICATION), 14, 29
intermediary's role and, 33, 35–36

NEW ENTRANTS (INTO MARKET), 68

NEW YORK INSURANCE DEPARTMENT, 73

NEW YORK REGULATION #98, 73

NEW YORK REGULATIONS #113 AND #114, 80

NO-FAULT AUTOMOBILE INSURANCE, 45

NON-TRADITIONAL REINSURANCE, 65

NORTH SEA PIPER ALPHA, 64

NOTE TO FINANCIAL STATEMENTS, 95

## O

OCCUPATIONAL DISEASE CLAIMS, 45

OCCURRENCE REINSURANCE AGREEMENT, 20, 23

OVERCAPACITY (IN REINSURANCE MARKET), 34

OVERUTILIZATION OF CAPITAL, 33

## P

PAST DUE AMOUNTS (RATIO TO TOTAL AMOUNT RECOVERABLE), 96

PHILOSOPHIES (OF COMPANY), 33, 36
claims audit and, 39
*See also* Management philosophy

PINK CASE (FIDELITY & DEPOSIT COMPANY VS. PINK), 72

PLACEMENT (BY INTERMEDIARY), 34–35, 72–73

POLICYHOLDERS' SURPLUS, 12, 15–17, 67
as key to financial health, 17
balancing accounts and, 18
conceptualization and, 33
*See also* Surplus penalty

POLLUTION, ENVIRONMENTAL, 61

POLLUTION EXCLUSION, 65

POOLS (REINSURANCE), 25–26, 91

POPULATION TRENDS, 62

PORTFOLIOS (OF REINSURANCE COMPANIES), 26

PREMIUM AND LOSS DATA
by line of business, 89
reporting, 88–92

PREMIUM VOLUME, 68, 74
for non–U.S. risks, 82
increasing, 15
*See also* Reporting premium and loss data

PREMIUM–VOLUME CAPACITY, 13, 32

PREMIUMS, RATIO OF SURPLUS TO, 17, 18

PRIMARY INSURANCE
 compared to reinsurance, 11, 12, 83
 mixed with pro rata and excess-of-
  loss, 90, 91
PRIMARY INSURANCE COMPANY
 claims department function in,
  37–38
 communication with reinsurer,
  35–36
 effect of reinsurance on, 11, 12, 14
 loss development patterns of, 37,
  51–58
 relationship with reinsurer, 27
 reporting of premium and loss data,
  89
 reserves vs. reinsurers' reserves, 69
 reserving practices of, 40
 risk exposure of, 60–64
PRIVITY OF CONTRACT, 63
PRO RATA (PROPORTIONAL)
 REINSURANCE, 19, 20–22, 26
 claims reporting and, 38
 financing and, 17
 mixed with excess-of-loss and
  primary, 90, 91
 reporting premium and loss data, 89
 reserving and, 40
 shift to excess form from, 64
PRODUCTION GOALS (OF COMPANY), 33
PRODUCTS LIABILITY, 45, 60
 efforts to reform, 64
PROFESSIONAL REINSURERS, 25, 27,
 68, 75
 two major methods of reporting by,
  90
PROFIT AND LOSS, REINSURANCE
 AND, 13
PROJECTION (OF LOSS COSTS), 40,
 42–43
 RAA study to aid, 51
PROPERTY COVERAGE, 60, 61
 annual statement requirements
  regarding, 88
 brokers and, 68
 pro rata reinsurance for, 19
PROPORTIONAL VS.
 NON–PROPORTIONAL
 REINSURANCE, 19, 89–90
PUBLIC HEALTH, 61

QUOTA-SHARE REINSURANCE, 20,
21–22, 26
 conceptualization and, 33

RATE FILINGS, 32, 33
RATE OF CLOSINGS, 33
REAGAN ADMINISTRATION, 70
RECEIVABLES, AGING OF, 72, 85, 95
RECIPROCITY, 26
RECOGNITION OF POTENTIAL
 UNRECOVERABLES, 95–97
RECOMMENDATIONS (BY
 INTERMEDIARY), 33
RECORDKEEPING (OF REINSURANCE
 TRANSACTIONS), 73
RECOVERABLE SCHEDULES, 72
REGULATION(S), 59, 83–86
 federal system of proposed, 74
 in the future, 86
 lack of, 73, 83, 84
 new, 72, 85
 See also Laws/legislation
REGULATORS, 94–95
 rising expectations of reinsurance
  industry by, 71–72, 84
REINSURANCE
 alien, 70, 77–82, 93
 availability of, 66, 74, 84
 beginnings of, 17
 behind-the-scenes nature of, 83
 benefits vs. cost, 14
 brokers. See Broker
 changes in environment of, 59–76,
  80–82, 84
 changing program of, 36
 cost–effective, 33, 34
 defined, 11
 financing increased by, 12, 15–17, 18
 forms/types of, 17, 19–23
 functions of, 12
 "partnership" nature of, 64
 primary insurance and, 11, 12, 14
 proportional vs. non-proportional, 19
 reasons why unfamiliar to many
  people, 11–12
 See also Reinsurance companies;
  Reinsurance departments;
  Reinsurance industry
REINSURANCE AND ANTI-FRAUD TASK
 FORCE, 84
REINSURANCE ASSOCIATION OF
 AMERICA (RAA), 42, 43, 87
 future studies of, 46

REINSURANCE ASSOCIATION OF
AMERICA LOSS DEVELOPMENT
STUDY, 37, 42–51
cautions regarding, 46–51
data derived from, 46
REINSURANCE COMPANIES
claims department function of,
37–40
disclosure among affiliate, 80
government-owned, 25
loss development patterns of, 37,
51–58
relationship with primary insurer, 27
reserves vs. primary company
reserves, 69
See also Reinsurance industry
REINSURANCE DEPARTMENTS (OF
PRIMARY COMPANIES), 25
REINSURANCE INDUSTRY, 25–27
changes in, 59–76, 80–82, 84
increased risk exposure in, 60,
63–66
professional reinsurers in. See
Professional reinsurers
rising expectations of, 71–74, 84
REINSURANCE INTERMEDIARY. SEE
BROKER; INTERMEDIARY
REINSURANCE LINE, 90, 91
REINSURANCE MARKET
effect of alien reinsurers on, 82
entry into, 68
fraudulent activity in, 84
increased size of ceding company
retentions and, 64
increasing competition in, 59, 67–69
international, 78
specialty companies and, 66
REINSURANCE MARKET/MARKETING,
26–27, 28–30
cycles in, 34, 65, 74, 88
intermediary's role and, 34, 35
REINSURANCE POOLS, 25–26, 91
REINVESTMENT RISK, 69, 71
REPORTED LOSSES, 40–41
early, 51
late, 46
See also Reporting claims; Reporting
premium and loss data
REPORTING CLAIMS, 38–40, 75
delay in, 52, 76. See also
Emergence, slow; Tail (of loss
development patterns)
reserving and, 40, 75

See also Reporting premium and loss
data
REPORTING PREMIUM AND LOSS
DATA, 88–92
RESERVE ADEQUACY, 33, 36, 97
as primary objective of actuaries, 51
RAA study to help estimate, 51
See also Reserving/reserves
RESERVING/RESERVES, 37, 40
actuary's report on needed amount
of, 41
analyses of, 38
case-basis, 39–40
cash-flow underwriting and, 69
claims department and, 38, 75
discounting for federal taxes, 71
for IBNR losses, 40
for latent injury cases, 46
long-tail, 51, 62, 69, 93
loss development patterns and, 42
regulators' concern about, 71
under-, 39, 91
unearned premium reserve account,
15
RETENTION
claims reporting and, 39, 42
excess-of-loss agreement and, 42
increased size of ceding companies',
64
indexing, 51, 70
lines and, 22
quota-share reinsurance and, 22
surplus-share reinsurance and, 20,
22
RETROCESSION, 26, 30
claims reporting and, 38
increasing frequency of, 46
surplus and, 67
RISK EXPOSURE, 59, 60–66
and less margin for error, 66–67
of alien reinsurers, 82
RISK RETENTION GROUPS, 66
RISK-BEARING CAPABILITY (OF
COMPANY), 33
RISK-SHARING MECHANISMS, 66

## S

S FUNDS, 94
SAMPLING (BY INTERMEDIARY), 32
SAVINGS AND LOAN ASSOCIATIONS,
69–70

SECURITIES AND EXCHANGE
COMMISSION, 91
SERVICE (BY INTERMEDIARY), 35–36
SHOCK LOSSES, 13
SHORT-TAIL LINES, 89, 92
SMALLER INSURANCE COMPANIES, 14,
38
  capacity gap between large
    companies and, 12–13
  direct market and, 30
  McCarran-Ferguson Act and, 74
SOCIAL INFLATION, 45
SOLVENCY REQUIREMENTS, 27, 83, 88
SPECIALTY COMPANIES, 66
STABILIZATION OF RESULTS, 13–14
  retrocession for, 26
STATE INSURANCE DEPARTMENTS, 35
STATEMENT PROTECTION, 33
STATISTICS/STATISTICIANS, 28, 38
STATUTORY ACCOUNTING, 70, 88
STOCK MARKET CRASH OF 1987, 69
STOP-LOSS CONTRACT, 23
STRICT LIABILITY, 60
SUBSCRIPTION, 34
SUNSET CLAUSE, 65
SURPLUS PENALTY, 93, 94, 95, 96
  calculation of, 97
  *See also* Policyholders' surplus
SURPLUS-SHARE REINSURANCE, 20–22
SURVEY (BY INTERMEDIARY), 31,
32–33
SURVIVOR BENEFITS, 46
SUSPECT RECOVERABLES, 94–95
SWISS RE, 78
SYNDICATES OR POOLS
(REINSURANCE), 25–26, 91

## ||||T

TAIL (OF LOSS DEVELOPMENT
PATTERNS), 42, 43
  short vs. long, 89, 92
  trend toward longer, 51, 62
TAX REFORM ACT OF 1986, 70
TAXES, 59
  alien reinsurers and, 80, 81
  federal, 70–71
  federal excise, 80
  state, 15
TECHNICAL SUPPORT, 38, 75
TECHNOLOGICAL ADVANCES, 60
TITLE INSURANCE, 88
TORT LIABILITY, 60, 61

governmental immunity from, 62
reform efforts concerning, 63, 64
TOXIC TORTS, 61
TRADING (REINSURED BUSINESS), 26
TREATY REINSURANCE, 19, 23, 26
  claims reporting and, 38
  vs. facultative, 63–64
  multiple–line, 90
  ratio to facultative, 27
  reserving and, 40
  shift from pro rata to excess forms,
    64
TRUST AGREEMENT, 80
TRUST FUNDS, 72, 84, 93
  maintained by alien reinsurers, 79

## ||||U

UMBRELLA INSURANCE, 42
UNAUTHORIZED INSURER, 93, 94, 95
UNDERCAPACITY (IN REINSURANCE
MARKET), 34
UNDERRESERVING, 39, 91
UNDERUTILIZATION OF CAPITAL, 33
UNDERWRITERS AT LLOYD'S, 78
UNDERWRITING, 12–13, 14
  account executives' role in, 30
  cash-flow, 69
  computers to aid, 75
  expertise in, 75
  intermediary's survey and, 32
  reserving and, 40
  staff for direct writing reinsurers, 28
UNDERWRITING AND INVESTMENT
EXHIBIT, 89, 90, 92
UNEARNED PREMIUM RESERVE
ACCOUNT, 15
UNRECOVERABLES, POTENTIAL, 95–97

## ||||V

VALUATION, 39, 40
  annual dates of, 52
VALUES
  geographic concentration of, 62
  rise in, 62

# ||| W

W FUNDS, 94
WASTE MATERIALS, 61
WITHDRAWALS, 65, 66, 68, 87
    new annual statement requirements
      due to, 94
WORDING, THE, 35
WORKERS' COMPENSATION CLAIMS,
    42, 89
    example of trend in, 48, 54, 57
    factors in changing patterns of,
      45–46
WORKERS' COMPENSATION
    REINSURANCE BUREAU, 25
WORLD MARKET, 60
WRITE-OFFS, 85, 95, 97

June 1989/5M/CC
Printed in U.S.A.